Praise for To the Chapel of Light

"I'm not convinced you want to read this. I mean, you're now in a motel on the side of the highway, blood on the walls, and this book is a note on a nightstand. Joshua Young has written a maddening book of clues that hang on to us until we crumble into the impossible joke of it. I got inside and tried to call you, but you didn't pick up. Young's phones are made of static. And there is no you. And there are no heroes. And an old birthday cake. A cow keeps rocking."

—Zachary Schomburg, author of *The Book of Joshua*

Praise for When the Wolves Quit

"A remarkable and delightful full-length debut, Joshua Young's *When the Wolves Quit* is a poetic Lynchian noir unlike any poetry before. Interrogating a familiar, provincial American space where 'secrets are damp, / caught in the space between the throat and the front teeth,' Young entices us to step onto the stage itself. ENTER STAGE LEFT: someone disappears. ENTER STAGE RIGHT: see the missing through a keyhole—or worse, through the slats of your neighbor's nearly closed blinds. Brilliantly suppressing distinctions between poetry, drama, and fiction, here is a frightening polyphony of voices, where all become victims of their own crimes—where 'suffering moves and breathes.' The smallest details are even more disturbing, such as an out of tune piano plinking over the debris of other people's lives in half-abandoned rooms. When told in the book this is dream, we think nightmare. Most worryingly, Young manages to implicate an audience who is much too titillated by the oblique violence happening offstage. Just try to remove yourself from that association, reader."

—Richard Greenfield, author of *Tracer* and
A Carnage in the Lovetrees

"In Joshua Young's *When the Wolves Quit*, the palpable influences of cinema and surrealism are woven together in this luminous play in verse. The firing of a gun triggers this emotional investigation of faith, memory, and the afterlife. With the same ferocity of a fired bullet Young's work accelerates the reader through his poetic obsession where the woods are ghostly and the path through the thicket is somewhere off the stage. With ingenuity and his strong gifts as a storyteller, Young's tale invites readers to become major characters and to explore a place that is the 'middle ground between closure and myth.'"

—Oliver de la Paz, author of *Requiem for the Orchard*

"Long after reading it, Joshua Young's *When the Wolves Quit* still sits on my chest heavy as stone, lapping at my throat with a sometimes tongue and the always threat of teeth. When I scream blood-lust for new words, this book is what I greedily nightmare about."

—J. A. Tyler, author of *The Zoo, A Going*

PSALMS FOR THE WRECKAGE

Published by Plays Inverse Press
Pittsburgh, PA
www.playsinverse.com

ISBN 13: 978-0-9914183-7-4

First Printing: May 2017
Cover design by Ryan Spooner
Page design by Tyler Crumrine
Printed in the U.S.A.

PLAYS
INVERSE

PSALMS FOR THE WRECKAGE

BY JOSHUA YOUNG

PLAYS INVERSE PRESS
PITTSBURGH, PA
2017

Dedicated to my loves:

Alexis
Elliot
Willa

TABLE OF CONTENTS

INTRODUCTION

Psalms for the Wreckage is a project years in the making. At first it was just a passing idea, but it grew into something more and more real as Tyler Crumrine and I worked together on my first title with Plays Inverse, *THE HOLY GHOST PEOPLE*. My first two scripts in verse—*To the Chapel of Light* and *When the Wolves Quit*—had gone out of print, and it felt right for Tyler to be the one to reprint them. They were the books that put me on his radar, and chatting about their themes online was what started our author/editor relationship. I also wanted to include something newish, though, to make the book a uniquely Plays Inverse publication rather than just another reprint. So with that in mind, I started reworking a third "play" to complete the *Psalms* trilogy: *This is the Way to Rule*.

To the Chapel of Light is a screenplay in verse, and *When the Wolves Quit* was my first play in verse, so my initial idea back in 2010 was to write a third book—a "symphony in verse." The result was a rambling 132 pages, but you can still see the remnants of some of the symphony's "movements" in *This is the Way to Rule*. Revisiting the drafts with Tyler in 2016, I decided to build a play out of the fragments, supported by interstitial letters similar to *Chapel* and *Wolves*. In the end, we were able to take the "old" writing and break it into something that stayed true to the original style, while also reflecting my growth as a writer over the years since.

I didn't really change direction so much as clarify what I had already put on the page, though. Back when this book was more a collection of poems than a play, I still used to build a scene in my head before throwing scraps of moments on the page to elicit feelings rather than plot. Transitioning to playwriting, I took these hypothetical scenes and built them into actual dialogue (sometimes) to allow a narrative unfold, however strangely it did.

Today *This is the Way to Rule* feels like a reaction to Trump, but it was initially written as a response to George W. Bush. The original symphony was triggered by a 2008 David Bazan song, "American Flags," about American flags getting tired of the direction the country is going in and what people do in their name. So they pull themselves off their flagpoles and swarm the White House, cornering the

President. In a way, this book was an exaggerated warning of what might happen without change. Thankfully Obama came along, but I had no idea that the book's scenarios—the fantasy of them, the darkness—would sound so relevant and appropriate in 2017. It sickens me to realize that this fantasy I created feels so familiar.

I wrote *To the Chapel of Light* first out of the three. It was my graduate thesis at Western Washington University, where Oliver de la Paz was my thesis advisor and really helped me find what *Chapel* was. I started writing *When the Wolves Quit* during a course I took on obsession & the long poem with Oliver as well, but finished it while at New Mexico State University thanks to the direction of Richard Greenfield. By the time I finished *Wolves*, pieces of *Rule* were already floating around in my head. Thanks to some tough love from Carmen Giménez Smith (and Richard), I started digging into the material in a way I hadn't before—*Wolves* and *Chapel* were clearly stories—and the lyric elements of *Rule* started to take shape.

Chapel is primarily about movement…about the places and people we don't see when we move through the country, especially places we've learned to forget. While much of it focuses on literal Middle America, the South, and Southwest, I was trying to use those landscapes to talk about more. I hope that comes across. The speakers cling to the idea that the end of their journey—the culmination of the passing landscapes—would somehow make everything make sense to them. It winds up becoming a kind of joke, though, since at the end of *this* there will never be real answers. The letters are marked "dear brothers."

Wolves is about trying to become stationary after moving and moving and moving. But there's no answer in that either. Instead, a newcomer finds darkness below the surface of a supposedly utopian town. The letters are marked "dear sisters."

Rule is my apocalypse book. Not post-apocalypse, but ongoing apocalypse. And the whole point was to see if I could find an ending. The letters are marked "dear survivors."

My twin brother recently asked if the letter writers were the same—I said they could be. These texts are definitely connected. In some ways part of me believes that in these books we are watching a world fall apart through the point of view of one person. I don't know how true that is, but I know it's possible.

Psalms for the Wreckage's three texts are a look back at when I first started using hybrid forms and post-genre approaches in my writing. I didn't know I was doing that at the time. I was just adapting poetry to all my years studying fiction and finding that both needed to be weirder, needed to be broken into pieces. And what happened were these little plays in verse (novels in verse / stories in verse). In each I was trying to write about an America I didn't know and still don't know. I was trying to understand, and the failure to find one genre, the failure to stop after one book, the failure to find answers at the end of these books, the failure to completely destroy the faith in these books, is why they still mean something to me. They're where I started learning how to write how I wanted to write and to start questioning things other than what those close to me were questioning. They're where I started noticing what I hadn't noticed before.

So here is this beast. It is ready for you to read as it was intended: one big book with three chapters—a trilogy of plays or play-like things trying to address faith, religious dogma, and the politics of power, published by a press whose mission statement complements the collection's form and content. I hope they mean something to you too, even if only a fraction of what they mean to me.

TO THE CHAPEL OF LIGHT

CAST OF CHARACTERS

Major Players

>the voyeurs
>the poet and his friend *(aka the poets)*
>the camera
>the brothers *(from the city)*
>the young priest
>the father
>the son *(aka the real son)*
>the spirit *(starts in the palms of the young priest)*
>the choir
>the young priest's mother
>the groom *(in the chapel of light)*
>the bride *(in the chapel of light)*

Minor Players

>radio broadcaster
>death
>heavenly creatures *(angels, god, etc.)*
>musicians
>followers
>assembly
>bootleggers
>the young priest's family
>all good thieves
>ghosts
>soldiers *(from the old and new wars)*
>children, women, and men *(met on the road)*

OVER BLACK
(V.O.)

"The cinema has given the death of Manolete a material eternity."
André Bazin, *Death Every Afternoon*

"The sun sank; all the roads were dark with shadows."
Homer, *The Odyssey*

"It is all dying out now in a voice asking,
Where you from? How ya'll folks doin'?"
Rodney Jones, *Elegy for the Southern Drawl*

"And how long would it take me to walk across the United States all alone?"
Jimmy Eat World, "Blister"

FADE IN

INT. APARTMENT – NIGHT

a poet comes to my door with snakes wrapped around his arms and says he's gonna pull a fiddle from the throat of a sparrow. no one believes him. his friend—another poet—makes everything worse, keeps saying, "i like it when a camera stops outside the door like this and just waits a moment, listens." and then, he tries to pull an organ from the speakers of the stereo.

rubbing the snakes wrapped around his arms, the poet says, "that's not what we came here for." and so the friend of the poet closes his eyes and opens his mouth to speak, but the words sound like mud sliding off a roof.

he clears his throat and waits a moment.

and then, he starts talking about the camera.

FADE TO BLACK.

ACT I

FADE IN

EXT. ROAD – MORNING

the voyeurs leave the city to find the chapel of light with nothing more than the road and a camera to follow.

EXT. ROAD – LATER THAT DAY

so, this is where it starts. the East Coast has vanished into the past and no one west of Georgia gives one fuck about New York, skyscrapers, mayflowers, or the ghosts of Roanoke.

and 'cause no one ever finds a cure at the waterfront, they'll turn towards the dirt and grain. sailors will wash to shore and wake just to make the long trudge into what's left of their cities, alone.

from here, you'll head west, almost always you'll head west. there's nothing back there except a death who hates her job and beggars who mean it when they say, "California is where you go to step on the toes of god."

out west somewhere lives a young priest with no hair, who found the spirit in the creases of his palms. he goes about touching the foreheads of who he thinks followers would call sinners, but the spirit in his hands is blind to sin and the whole show never works how it's supposed to.

instead, boys and girls with blue eyes kick and foam at the mouth while their foreheads burn, and these rooms get cut open by shafts of light from windows and scripture hum.

CUT TO:

dear brothers,

no, we did not get a map, but we nodded as if what they said were lines and x's drawn on paper, something that could guide us. before they left, the poet said, "the road is not your friend. no matter what you see or hear, it is simply a guide, or maybe you can look at it as the tracks hunters follow to the watering hole. so, follow it, but do not trust it. it might leave breadcrumbs to keep you lost, but only follow its sound and movement, not ever what it has left behind."

so, here we are chasing…what?

places, peoples, ghosts, and halves of stories.

INT. CAR – DAY

the radio dial turns from static to fuzz, and there's the voice of a preacher, or maybe not a preacher, maybe just a man who has something to say. and he speaks, continues...

what should you do?

...look, if you push hard enough, you'll see the whole thing turn to stone. 'cause here everyone wants to settle up, tear the roots from the dirt, and give the blacktop that old rubber and exhaust. you couldn't really call it traveling so much as a kind of hand washing, or the tearing out of pages. we were born anchors and you will drag against the state line, only half-fracturing the distance between home and "out there" 'cause home just threads itself deep into the skin, but you'll keep saying, "we'll get there somehow."

CUT TO:

the east keeps calling, pulling
up from the shoulders, trying
to heave the Carolinas up into
their cities, but the lights already
keep them warm. they have kept
the rust of automobiles moving
southwest, to keep the breath alive.

EXT. COUNTY ROAD – EARLY EVENING

here, you'll find it tethered between two towns shaped like vases. there are cattle farms and old automobiles sitting on roadsides. there's a stench—quiet at first—that will make weaker men keel over. you'll smell it when you read the pavement just right. that's how you'll know you're where you're supposed to be.

all those gothic pillars at the front of white plantation houses. there are miles of them with American flags in the center of lawns as though it actually says something about freedom and pride. at the end of blocks, street signs pass like pages can turn in novels, except fingers won't cut on corners and dresses won't parachute in the wind. if you keep moving, there are children at bus stops, at street edges, at the elbow of town, by factories, waiting, staring at their hands in the sunlight.

behind stained glass, they've piled bricks and bolted doors to lock cowboys in confessionals to look their sins right in the eye. once that happens they're changed, fixed, or maybe broken. at least what happens stays in the confessionals.

you won't find anything whimsical down here. no skipping or dancing on wooden floors, or even a goddamned smile, unless it's at the tight end of a rope, or in the scars of a cross fire, or even the swallow of well water in the late summer months. two conversations can take place if you must have them. one involves words i dare not repeat. the other? words such as faith, salvation, and the second coming, but only ends with the spray of holy water and loose shoulders.

in winter, birds arrive in clumps and park their bodies in trees above the house. old men, long past due, smoke pipes on the front steps of family cabins. they are the last of those families. death has long since skipped their names on his list. their skin has started to turn like banana peels and wet leather. they've already buried their wives in backyards like pets, and hammered crosses with initials carved into their centers.

CUT TO:

dear brothers,

so, you're at loose ends with it all? imagine if a camera was there, hand-held, as if it was stitched into the moment to hover and watch. there, no one can touch without that dull ache of work like a tower never rescued.

all those books and books like filled parking spaces and silences where something cold and damp gets caught between, sort of waiting to be taken.

remember how he used to stand in the room and stare at his children like he was reading a map, while they half-eyed him, half-smirked, blinking like the flip of light switches?

when they talk to each other the space between their bodies swells; conversations Hemingway would kill for, those hills-like-white-elephants carry on and mumble, only there's Coca-Cola and cigarettes perched between fingers.

a family like that will always silhouette itself in doorways. those are the things we have learned from windowsills and curtains.

EXT. HIGHWAY – NIGHT

from the highway you can see the asylum down in the valley, dug into the northern half of the bog. everything is dead, or rotting, or working its way there. the walls stand half-erect, foundation sinking to the left. window bars, tattoos, and faces behind them, eyes half-closed. this is where they keep the musicians who couldn't let the cotton field songs die. they're still singing in the cells, all through the dark.

when people tell you there's no jazz in heaven, just know they are liars. god's up there with his gold and angels, and probably he's got his eyes closed as he listens to all that trumpet riff and tap, tap.

that's why no one ever gets what they prayed for.

it's the blues you won't find behind the pearly gates. angels' wings would start dropping from the clouds and everyone would become sunsets dying.

god sticks with jazz. the blues gets reserved for the shadows of roadside bars and farmhouses miles from town, or the faded jukeboxes that haven't been paid or fingered in years. and when it actually plays, everyone gets one chance to feel the phantom limbs of America.

CUT TO:

dear brothers,

so, we lost ourselves pretty quick with all that music blaring,
but we never had to ask directions. on a bathroom wall we
found a note in chalk:

> move past the hammer
> that bends into the sea.
> the camera only goes
> down there for backstory
> and a good laugh. this is not
> the time for that. if you really
> want humor keep moving west
> past the clay and sulfur into what
> everyone calls California.
> —*the poet*

and on we go, pointing ourselves south, and just a bit to
the west.

EXT. APARTMENT – MIDDAY

the grown-ups in this town are bodies on the clothesline, just shirts filled with wind. they snake and soar in alleys.

and the men rub their fingers against the palms of each other just to feel blood pulsating like a parade of children. eyes glide across the surfaces of things like they're playing with fingers, or masquerading as nerves, or maybe just cobwebs.

droplets quiver as a spider spins.

and the women used to get around, walking around, trying to find clues for all the mysteries and mistakes god had made, as if these things could speak of something to speak of. eyes drift over roots choking half-standing walls. an old birthday cake dumped by the roots of a tree.

droplets quiver as a spider spins.

there's a notebook lying alone, beside the couch someone left. inside, a child scribbled, "they were never kids like us, they had worked in wars and built machines. they had trouble finding any peace. do you know how that feels?" and this. this thought stings like barbed wire. it unfolds them all like newspapers or children's books. they try to remember what it felt like back then, before, but the men were too busy pounding steel for the railroad company, the one slowly dying.

and there. a white dove. a black face next to a brick building, profiled, walking about the skyline. the old rusted water tower across town that hasn't been used in years. and now, drunk as a shithouse rat, running fingers along the bars of a fence.

droplets quiver as a spider spins.

CUT TO:

EXT. GAS STATION – EARLY EVENING

at a gas station, a woman from the city says, "i love your accent," to the man holding the pump.

the man says, "down here, you can't call it an accent, you have to say, 'drawl.'"

CUT TO:

dear brothers,

we meet the poet and his friend in a room without windows.
they stay huddled in corners opposite, without speaking, till
the room is so silent we can hear blood coursing. the poet
rises, looks around, says, "we got our hands on a map. it ain't
done yet, but we got the rest coming."

"what about the choir?" the friend says. "warn them of the
choir."

outside, a train moans six blocks over, gulls scatter preaching
gospels of the city, and the snakes wrapped around his arms
start slithering, squeezing, choking. he rubs them and they
calm. "oh yes, the choir will pull you off course if you let it.
do not let it call to you. do not listen if it does. those voices
do not sound like the road, that's how you'll know when not
to listen. my friends, you must only listen to what the road
tells you."

at the door, they turn to smile.

the poet salutes, and he and his friend disappear into the
alley as though they're crawling out of caves.

EXT. FARM – DAY

sometimes there's blood in the dirt, but only when it comes to blows and shotgun spray. "property. this whole fucking thing is about property," a boy says, gripping the shotgun when the bank man comes to collect, but there's nothing left. a cow keeps rocking in place, behind the barn, but she's just skin and bone and a little guts. they'd cook her later if she wasn't so thin.

and out across the road, the hill keeps chewing men, slack-jawed and hungry. "i'll just slow you up," one says. god, how they all speak in drawls. at the river's edge men bleed from the tree line like water from a paintbrush. the blood will not be used to clean, but to close eyes and sleep.

CUT TO:

dear brothers,

after that whole mess, we left Memphis-bound and gagged.

INT. LIVING ROOM – NIGHT

the young priest's sister would get drunk on gin and recall her dreams.
sitting at the edge of his bed, she'd say things, things like,

> "there's a shack in the middle of a lake,
> where escapees lay their heads
> when the chase is close, bodies sunk
> at the corner. no one from the law
> ever really finds them."

CUT TO:

dear brothers,

as we move, that line slacks across the horizon, keeps pulling at what's left of the light. no sleek edges of skyscrapers. here, it's all sun and reflection, or maybe gold buried in the ground. and in the distance they stand calling from rocks and water for skin and nerve-static, or maybe just bodies to stitch into what's left of the south.

all that dirt-road kick-up and follow-through collects like the patter of feet gathering up a staircase. listen to the hiccup of the body's lust for a soft spot to lay itself, and we should not answer their calls from rocks, we should not shed our clothes like shucking corn. we pull ourselves anyway, towards that choir.

EXT. PARK – DAY

out before the horizon spreads, an old man keeps preaching about the new floods and the bursting and building of dams. but he doesn't remember that if you reach the ocean by sunup, and turn to face the land, a camera might be there to move in and hold. catch all that western dying light, the last hope for that one American dream that keeps tugging at the shirt sleeve of your jacket. but now, there's nothing to stop the fall, just a curtain slowly drooping into darkness. you'll still remember the light, 'cause the sun left spots in everyone's eyes.

CUT TO:

EXT. COURTYARD – MORNING

there are patterns waiting to take you into the morning, and you'll fit right there with the bird chirps and engine muster. and settle. this poison is not bottled or spoon-fed, but cut right from the teeth of your neighbors' son as he screams, "i killed a man and no one can touch me for it!" he shakes like beetle wings.

and across town someone else keeps dancing, as if there is a flashback with lighting through a window above the sink. all those fingers over the silk of a dress. later, the camera doesn't cut when the letter comes, and wreckage retreats from the sockets of soldiers as they read.

CUT TO:

dear brothers,

yes, i remember the exit.

the friend of the poet stood in the doorway, picking at a missing chip from the frame. he looked at the poet and said, "someone needs a touch up," and "this looks like a junebug on fire." the poet only grinned and said, "that's not what we're here for."

so, the friend of the poet straightened himself and started clicking out words, "the camera waits in places, usually it's dark like hallways and smells of blood or soldier musk, but if there's enough light it'll catch the action."

everyone grinned, 'cause he was talking about the camera again.

what happens when you talk
about freedom—some people
would kill to prove they have
it. this right here is the birth
of two thousand plateaus
and trailer park rust.

EXT. DINER – MORNING

a postcard finds them by morning. it's only a picture of the sky, cloudless.

> you can meet us
> in the city that
> choked.
> —*the poet*

CUT TO:

INT. CHURCH – NOON

here, the assembly stays drunk on the blood that's supposed to be the lamb, but they keep the doors shut to the real son and listen only to the words that they find kicking from their own guts, from their own teeth.

listen: the sounds of the son's fists against the doors and the lies that spill out of their throats.

CUT TO:

EXT. PORCH – NIGHT

the young priest's mother, crooked from child after child, would sneak into his room, listen to the night outside his window, and whisper in the dark,

> "have you heard of the gate that opens
> into the folds of America?
> people pass through just to watch skin
> unfold, and cities burn."

CUT TO:

where the rails meet the road
blood drips on the pavement.
a mother waits for the white
sheet to darken her face.

EXT. WOODS – MAGIC HOUR

the trees here keep singing out, begging to be cut and cleared like a saxophone sweeping all the scales in the key of d. and a beat keeps it steady, coming from a hammering behind the gravedigger's cabin.

if she could speak, she'd tell you to stay out in the thicket just to hear conversations about sin and god between stray locusts and the first born of small towns. both will smile without teeth and laugh without breathing, but she'd insist you'd know what they mean.

CUT TO:

INT. BAR – NIGHT

there are men with beards and dunlaps, always smoking rolled cigarettes and drinking unmarked whiskey on the covered porch of the town bar.

they watch the road for people they don't know or pale horses or the pastor's freckled wife on her afternoon walk.

and inside, there is only one kind of beer to go with the one kind of whiskey and not even the bartender knows the brand. confederate ghosts claim the back room where the lights haven't worked in ages. they stay there 'cause the light only reminds them of what they really are. the dust back there is so thick you need a broom just to walk.

they sing to each other, songs about the war and their wives. the dust hovers and spins when they sing. you can't hear them over the twang from jukeboxes and bar chatter, glass clink and aftertaste.

in the bathroom, someone has carved lines into walls from books Jordan and Jones wrote like, "a town is the size of language" and "because somewhere a bird clutches the scrap of my name." and of course, these speak to the men who enter, call names at them, tell them stories about the south.

CUT TO:

EXT. STORE – DAY

the storefront has gathered a handful of teens with faces burnt by outside jobs and shadeless porches, and one says,

> "all that comes
> through is a train
> every three hours.
> it passes through
> as though there's
> nothing to pass."

CUT TO:

INT. CAR – DAY

the channels keep coughing and cutting out one by one, into the fuzz…

what will they say?

…they might mention something about the holy spirit and honesty, but that's just the part of the tongue that spits out vowels and saliva like exclamation marks. if you really want to get through it all, you'll find him loose and ready to listen in the diner near the lake, eyeing the base of a bottle like it was some kind of fucking ghost looking back at him.

CUT TO:

EXT. THE CITY THAT CHOKED – NIGHT

when you've passed the turn-around—
all the foundations here are cracked, the pipes have rusted
      through
and morticians love to light cigarettes when they finish cutting
      and sewing—

this place only breathes in, inhaling what comes from the road.

    this is the city that choked.

FADE TO BLACK.

ACT II

FADE IN

INT. DINER – EVENING

the poets offer a map—the voyeurs must fill in the blank spaces between points.

to the chapel of light:

if you start at the road leading up to the armory, you can hear the followers off in the trees, around a fire, dressed in dirty white, singing about god's wrath and love, and how it all coincides with the washing of sins. if you look east at dark you can see the flicker of their fire like a candle in the belly of a whale.

they keep pulling at the wire leading to the shoreline as if it is attached to the toes of god, or at least some kind of monster waiting to sink its teeth. but the wire is nothing more than a guideline for failure, or a path to salt, or even a string to sand where strangers dance on the roofs of rusted cars like they just saw the pale horse descend into the fields across town.

here is the fork, the section in the road that leads to sin or Arkansas. one way is all ghost towns and dead soldiers lined up on the roadside with air for arms, smiling like the ripping away of wallpaper. old men wander between buildings, talking about how they don't ever want to draw, but the pistol keeps dry-fucking them with every step towards the crossroads. and the other way is twenty-somethings in all-night cafés talking about the difference between love and lust, and it's lip smack and slow-dancing in the corner of the bar to ignore the jukebox's clatter and hum.

you will not know which way is which until the fire starts.

if you listen you can hear the silence rubbing itself against blades of grass. follow the compass east to find the kids at the top of the tower, all stone and iron. there are windows, but no glass to stop the plunge. across the trail, due south, there's a dungeon in the side of a hill that we can call the belly. they keep the ghosts of storytellers in there, like Owen, Twain, Steinbeck, Faulkner. these ghosts pound from the inside, but their fists are too soft to make a sound. and you'd only admit to knowing them by name and not by the ink they've left behind.

"you could be my Amsterdam," he'll say when you're lying there waiting for the next sentence. blinking lights and sweat and culture. but he doesn't mean Amsterdam, he means Mobile, Alabama, before ten a.m., where there are boards on the windows and dust gathering everywhere. there is not an ocean separating you from that place, just the stretch of highway and grain, and maybe dead grass.

there are scarecrows lined up like telephone poles at the gettin' place, and behind them, by the clumps of dirt and stone, you'll find the parts of mailboxes left in piles as if they are bones. a wolf oversees the graveyard as though these pieces were once her children. wives will watch this through screen doors. and over the hill anyone can find gulls pulling worms from the sand and seaweed.

they'll make you quit speaking with fists. instead, they'll expect sparks to spring from your skin with every touch, but not like a lover's touch, more like knives against the blacktop in winter. look, you can see their breath exit the car window like cats from alleyways, or men from a grave. they'll make your hands into calluses without nerves so that you can't really feel the weight of a moment when you hold it in your palms.

rotary drunk dials from couches to daughters. the voice on the other end will speak only in whispers. the meaning of these conversations will be found, years later, after the fall, in houses along the Mississippi, filled with empty bottles lined up like junkies in a kitchen.

magic hour is purgatory, only there ain't no flames when you reach the end.

there are lines and lines of a-frames. sometimes, soldiers from the old war appear at the edge of the tree line as if they are about to jump. at night, they're still out there in the pitch. you can hear them if you really listen.

the chapel of light is a shack on a farm, behind a lake that isn't blue. weddings are lit by candles and never end. god is not there. even his son avoids it. it's the damp air inside that turns them away. it'll stick on you for decades.

FADE TO BLACK.

FADE IN

EXT. DESERT ROAD – MORNING

the voyeurs will find the young priest and move on, towards the chapel of light.

INT. CAR – DAY

again, the channel starts going, and with a turn of the dial it narrows into something audible…

what does this show?

…it shows us what he is, like a camera might catch lens flare or a reflection of itself in windows. but here is where you should follow the rails into the gut of the hillside. he'll grin at you like headlights on a train and cut the sickness from your throat because you are not a warrior, not the forgotten, not the one hidden under the floorboards. you're closer to those tweakers on Gunn avenue, keeping at the glass. you'll hang around porches like inside is the last game in town, and there's practically blood on your lips. you might wave a cigarette around like a roman candle or a fishing pole.

CUT TO:

dear brothers,

no, it didn't take much to convince, us did it? two cool-
looking poets spitting prophecies or hellish tongues of the
old word. truth is, we just want to be heroes. it's that simple
and spelled out.

just off the highway
isn't really a town
so much as a gas station
and one motel. so, these sons
and daughters spend
their lives loving strangers for days,
or even hours, at a time.

EXT. HILLSIDE – EVENING

in the outskirts, there's salt in the water, but not an ocean for miles. the town hides the roads leading there, as though it were some kind of trespassing vein. no one ever finds the town, 'cause no one ever finds the road. it's all gravel and grass, and looks like a dead end. the families there stand under dead trees tearing at their skin as though they could lift the sunlight from their hands.

boys from the outskirts always stop their cars to kick the roadkill. once, they found a young girl from the Midwest rolled into a ditch. for some reason, they just reached out and moved her hair out of her eyes and watched her lay still. it wasn't until nightfall when they picked her up and drove.

they found the town, but not because they were looking, 'cause they were trying to find an ocean to bury the girl. they buried her, but never left. they built homes on the cliff hanging over the ocean, and lived there talking about returning home until they were too old to actually do it. they all died there, on the cliff. left their bones to settle.

no, you won't find a camera here. there's nothing inside houses and shacks but shovels and furniture, sometimes bodies. you won't even find photographs on walls. people grew sick of how young everyone used to be. you can find pieces and piles of cameras by the willow trees if you follow the trail up to the overhang. they're rusted by now, maybe strangled by weeds and warped from sun and water. sometimes, the youngest ones here pick at the piles and wonder what these used to be, but that question only lasts half a year.

CUT TO:

EXT. HIGHWAY – EVENING

this is not Iowa. Iowa is the place to peel back cornfields or maybe just sink into them to feel awake. between it all, you can find strips of concrete with chunks removed to hide the keys to the locks opening the west. hundreds of drunks show up to fish the holes. when they catch what they want, they move out and claim what they can.

here, men pile up to throw stones at sinners and clasp their hands around pistols as if one squeeze of a trigger is the last way to show your country's love. nothing is meant to kill, the joke just ends up going too far north.

CUT TO:

EXT. RIVER – MORNING

down in the shallows, beyond the covered bridge, there's the young priest with holes where his eyes should be. he lost them to the bootleggers, still looking for gas money and a ticket west. now he wades there all day, telling stories about the west and women and foxes and spiders, and how everyone here bleeds America or just the echoes of something left over from wars and crusades.

but the riverbed and rocks don't listen.

hell, no one really listens, 'cause all anyone can hear is the flapping of wings—everyone is either a vulture or blood drained from a pedestal, and no matter which, all these two ever do is circle and plunge.

he screams, "i got a knife and i know how to use it!"

CUT TO:

dear brothers,

"we are the romans," the priest says from the shallows and points to the top of the hill. but we cannot see through the fog and sunlight. he says he saw the camera pushing up the hill, into a close-up. but it could've been a horse, or a soldier returning from the dirt. like every time the wind blows it echoes and carries and keeps things cool.

all these telephone poles lead into the hearts of cities and concrete. this is where letters go to die, now nothing more than trash-fillers and things that lead to static.

that's why these keep coming to you, to keep this all alive.

EXT. BORDER – DAY

you will hate the way it smells when the borderline passes. cloves, gulf water, and chicken meat, all on fire. you might stop as though there's something to watch, though there's nothing but highway and empty houses.

if you run your fingers through the dead grass and peel back what you know about privacy, you'll know exactly where you've been led. keep saying, "this belongs to me" when you touch the ends of empty shotgun shells. when you do this, your purpose will be clear.

the last of the motel chronicles were drawn on napkins, left in drawers next to bibles, and the skeletons of station wagons jammed between rocks and tree stumps keep slowing you down. missionaries at pit stops fill up on what pieces of god they can pull from the pews. that's what they need to spread the word where John Ford left his fingerprints.

CUT TO:

INT. ROADSIDE DINER – AFTERNOON

inbetween a couple of half-laughs, this leathered-out old man with a sneer for a smile spits through his front teeth and waves out at the road. he says,

> "rest stops are really
> just parts of America no
> one gives a fuck about."

CUT TO:

dear brothers,

yes, the poets were clear about it all, about the chapel of light.

we remember what was said: "the wedding is like a handshake between fathers, only there's blood at the end and piles of caskets and shallow graves. when their hands part, skies will open up, dropping salt on the earth. we cannot go there ourselves to end it. we can only draw a map. you are still young enough to make the trek across the asphalt and dirt. the camera will be there to record and they will be there, waiting like stones on a riverbank. do not look into their eyes when you get there."

you ask as though we weren't convinced that this is what we want.

INT. CAVES – NIGHT

in the caves of clay and water, every thief from Allgood, Alabama, has gathered, bunkered up in the caves on the far side of the river. they came to trade blades and talk about the spiders they've come to fear. they sit on the cusp of shit they won't admit is coming for them. the sky has turned yellow and white, and the grass has turned to salt. but they cannot see. they sit in the caves and trade and talk and sometimes tell stories.

CUT TO:

INT. ABANDONED RAILROAD STATION – EARLY EVENING

further along, nobody knows what to do, so they ride the rails. these are the places the road sometimes swallows. there are farms without men or women, just children to plow and cut. their hands have become bricks shedding red dust into the fields like ladybugs or locusts, and all day they make the sounds of swinging and pulling tools, only they make them with their mouths, 'cause everything else is so quiet.

sunsets call them to bed and they sleep as though there is no morning.

CUT TO:

INT. WOODSHED – MORNING

the young priest's uncle used to smoke cigarettes, one after another, always smirking, always telling stories. one Christmas, he said,

> "there's an ark in the middle
> of a field stacked full of rocks
> and newspapers. the builders
> know it won't float if the flood
> comes, but they follow
> what god suggests."

CUT TO:

EXT. CLIFFSIDE – DAY

there are grain silos at the far end of the state, where the last of the American dragons have come to rest. there is no fire left, only scales and wings. and everyone calls a bar a "pub," even though the Irish have long since retreated back to Boston. inside, the long pregnant silences between tables and bodies shake. and every parent here loves the oil derrick shadows and grain debris. they wait to live through their sons' first wars, just so they can read the family name in newspapers or graveyards. and the youngest girls climb onto crosses, wishing they were that one son.

CUT TO:

INT. KITCHEN – MORNING

this is one of the parables the young priest's father said at breakfast tables:

> "have you heard the story about
> the kid who stands in the middle
> of a field with roots for feet?
> his mother feeds him three
> meals a day, and he talks about
> the camera he keeps seeing pass
> by every few years."

CUT TO:

INT. GAS STATION – DAY

an old man, with a hunk of chaw shoved into the valley of his mouth, yawns and says,

> "the rain here
> is desperate.
> it claws
> at the earth,
> but only sinks
> and hardly
> leaves a trace."

CUT TO:

EXT. MOUNTAIN ROAD – DAY

the coda drags everyone back thirty miles at a time, and the dust keeps kicking up as though coughing, adopting windshields and skin.

the next set of hills, miles from here, hold windmills, but they have stopped breathing and waving their arms at the ones passing by. and just over the hill where they stand, there are rocks, corrugated iron everywhere, for homes and playgrounds. they spread like blackberries.

the stretch ahead is empty, like one ever needs prayer again, 'cause the son came back for the rapture somewhere in Arizona, and he's knee deep in heathens and indians.

CUT TO:

INT. HOSPITAL – NIGHT

the old hospital doors are mouths. they continue to eat the wounded and poor left from the war, stay shut when the sick from down the street show, and tell the rich that the side entrance is a better place to find help. nurses take turns sleeping in hallways leading to the morgue.

here, when you die, you die. there are no ghosts, or spirits, or afterlife, just dirt and dark and funeral plans.

the men speak in lyrics of the late Hank Sr. and all his vinyl glory.

there are maps carved into the tree line, offering a way into the heart of what's left of this country, but the bark starts to tear itself away when anyone looks at it, as if it's ashamed of what it is there for. if you step back far enough, you can see where it leads, but only when the moonlight breaks through and cuts across the front. at the end, where it's been marked by an X, there's a talking snake handing out maps to Arkansas and heads of lettuce. at the stone's head, where the names have been chiseled, the camera will focus.

listen: there's the sound of hearse clank and rattlesnake bones.

the difference between cemeteries and shallow graves lies at the river's mouth.

the church elder's daughter scribbles what she remembers of the old testament onto the hands of mothers.

that's what gets done in doorways.

CUT TO:

to borderlines, where Mexico
waits for the tired, the ones who
have lost their laugh to modern
things like planes and stoplights,
the Southwest keeps pulling
them back into the desert.

INT. CAR – DAY

and again the static comes on like the cutting of cords and the bending of metal. adjust again, away from the fuzz...

where should we go?

...first thing's first, climb down off that soapbox and look him in the eye when you speak about things he never really wanted to hear. finger out the rust stuck between your teeth and cut your losses at the ankles. it's the only way you'll ever convince anyone that you should be where you're trying to stand. it's all a joke anyway, 'cause no one gives a fuck enough to really say otherwise, so no matter what soapbox you climb off of, there's still another one waiting, like a step.

CUT TO:

dear brothers,

we can see it from this place. the air tastes like whiskey and snow, but the summit is warm and dry enough to sit on the ground. the chapel is down there, behind the lake, light popping from its every crease and opening like the earth just opened its shutter. and there's a procession of ghosts and soldiers spread all the way to the foot of what we stand on. the water leading towards the lake has started to boil and turn brown, and all the soldiers keep kneeling to scald what's left from their bones. they want to be naked, just bones.

the poet and his friend did not warn us of this, but i can see god down there with his son, camped out on the far end of the next pass that leads into the musk and cold of a city, barely breathing. they watch the procession and the son bites his father's nails.

the young priest is there with them, in front of a fire, trying to burn the spirit from his hands. it's not the wind we can hear howling through the pass. it's the voice of the spirit begging for mercy, begging to stay put, deep in the creases of the priest's palms.

DÉNOUEMENT

FADE IN

EXT. THE CHAPEL OF LIGHT – MORNING

DELETED SCENE

at the chapel of light

i.

the camera starts for the inside, pushes itself across the threshold,
past all the loose skin and blood of ghosts and soldiers.
the front door has been opened and the inside of the chapel weeps.
from here, you can hear god telling his son to find the spirit—
now is not the time to be unaccounted for. last night is still fresh
to him, when the spirit got drunk on river blood and started
shouting,
"get back on the cross, that's all you're good for!"
and really, last anyone heard,
the spirit had made its way to Montana
by sunup, and someone saw him jumping off the backs of cattle.

the son finds the young priest at the river
at a spot cold enough to cool his hands.

ii.

the camera keeps pushing in,
through the door,
and inside,
no one looks.
the clicking sounds more
like a group of children
singing,
"salvation will come, salvation will come,"
or foxes speaking
in tongues.
this is probably why the son
keeps holding his hand
over his mouth
and laughing.

inside
there they are standing.

the room dampens
when their gazes meet,
as though the room
has coughed.
the light expands
like blood on bandages.

iii.

and on conversations of skin
he forks his fingers at the tremble

of flesh on her neck. watching it twist
like ink dropped into a bowl of water.

and the way her wrists go slack
at the warmth of his skin and the dead

whispers he breathes into her ear,

"inside me there is a room no one will penetrate. its windows are
shuttered and its doors have been nailed to frame."

now, it's her turn to touch him,
so she draws her finger across

the lump of his shoulders and blinks
at the candle flicker. sweat gathers

in the small of her back and breathes
like fire alarms pulled,

like the skin around his thigh
as if it was dipped in tar.

and she speaks as though
this is the last of it,

"i have duplicated the ripe twist of a fire built to silhouette
those bodies waiting to enter the cave where blood shapes

flesh, wet and guarded by folds of creased skin they will burn
in their lust burn like the ones before."

iv.

those who have been inside will know where
the chalk outlines of American gods have been.

if you look close enough, the marks are still there, just barely.

this is when you must enter,
cross the threshold
and take the camera in your hands.
it will get to the first outline—
the one four pews back, barely
the shape of a spider.
this is when you must turn it off.

it is not a simple switch flip or button push.
no. it must be final.
the film must be exposed,
the lens must be cracked.

this is when the air
will snuff out the candles,
that's how you'll know.

and if you make it out, lock the doors—
block them if you have to—
just to keep everything you left inside.

this is when you start the fire.
match, lighter, spark,
they will burn if you ask them to.
let it, until you can kick its ashes
when it cools.

this is when the voices will stop.

you won't find a pale horse,
or angel wings,
or even fucking trumpets,
but you'll find the poet and his friend
on the summit,
slouched by a fire.

this is where they'll be waiting for you.

FADE TO BLACK.

WHEN THE WOLVES QUIT

CAST OF CHARACTERS

Major Characters:

> The Preacher (#523)
> The Guilty Boys
> > The Quiet One (#521)
> > The Guilty One (#522)
> Kasey
> The Sheriff
> The Letter Writer
> The Preacher's Brother
> The Congregation

Minor Characters (Selected):

> The Deputies
> The Letter Writer's Sisters
> The Lovers (Deceased)
> The Congregation
> The Elders
> The Elders' Daughters
> The Girl Who Survived the Ghost Woods
> The Captured Ones
> Wolves
> The Parade of Ghosts (aka The Bodies)
> The Drunk
> The Mayor
> The City Sharks

The Names on the List (Selected):

> Kaveh Smith (#17)
> Dawn Smith (#18)
> Douglas McGuire (#19)
> Ruth Collins (#20)
> Russell Lee (#21)
> Emily Northrup (#27)
> Oliver Northrup (#28)
> Thomas Hansen (#41)
> Kathryn Hansen (#42)

No Corresponding Name (#58)
No Corresponding Name (#59)
No Corresponding Name (#147)
No Corresponding Name (#148)
Bruce Powell (#155)
Dicky Green (#171)
Samantha Green (#172)

gunshots.

sometimes, at night, when the wolves quit.

there.

a gun's going off deep in the thicket, coming out of the canyon.

once it was two lovers who couldn't touch each other anymore.
their parents found them out the sunday prior—called them
sinners, faggots, said things they shouldn't've meant. so these two
boys took from their fathers and walked through the meat of town,
into the woods, and down into the canyon. the air wasn't warm,
or cold, but thick and heavy. it smelled of topsoil and syrup. the
blonde one shot first, then took himself. no one knew till easter,
and their names were crossed off the list. by then the birds had got
to them, nothing left but un-edible.

another time, it was a hunter from the city
trying to find his way back
to the road.
he found a gray mass along the way,
but after the echo
cleared,
all he saw of it
was a thick chunk
of fur
and a few specks of blood.

tonight, the blasts come in pairs. it wasn't too far away. if you
listened, you could hear
                        whispers.

"should we?"

                                      and

"no, he can bleed where he is."

there's a commotion coming from the church.

SPOTLIGHT CENTER STAGE – SUNDAY, 8:00 A.M.

this town is built on the vanishings.
it's part of everyone's story.

there's a list for each name—
it's tacked to the wall under the clock in the sheriff's office.

the preacher disappears.
no one notices till the church service sunday,
when the pews fill up,
and the sermon never comes.

from the pews,
a rumble of whispers begin sometime in the silence,
and rumors swell like a new bruise.

smiles creep up faces. some frown
and some keep their lips
and only listen to what gets said.

the preacher's brother took two elders
down the block to the preacher's house and came back
saying there was no answer at his door.
inside his bed is unmade
and there's probably a week's worth of dust on things.

someone mentions the ghost woods.
that gets the congregation praying.

LIGHTS UP

dear sisters,

our town hasn't changed much since i've been in the eastern cities. all the old places i used to go with you and my friends are still around—that rope swing over the river, that sandy nook over the wash.

it's been months since we saw each other and i know i promised to stay in touch, but after we said goodbye, i followed the river out of the neighborhood, down to the tracks, and headed west. it took a day to catch an open boxcar and i rode that for a handful of days before ending up here. i didn't plan on staying, but i was hungry and wandered into town. by the time i got back to the rails, the train had left. i gave up waiting after a day.

i found a room above the general store that's got a view of half the town, from the orchard to the gloomed woods at the edge of town that i've heard people call the ghost woods. people say it claims those who wander inside—gathers them up when they breach the tree line.

ENTER STAGE RIGHT – THE PREACHER

yes, this town had a preacher,
young and tan in his day,
who used to preach of answers in arches,
answers in brick, in towers.

he'd spit sermons from the pulpit,
dressed in white
and black, weaving his hands
through the air in front of him
as if he was slapping the devil away.

some people said he took money from the offering plate
to fill his belly and pay his debts—

these city sharks kept moving,
finding him in the basements
of pubs, hugging barrels like the last
raft in water, in the alley
behind the station at midnight,
conversing with the lines of white
on the building, or at the grocery store's
window staring
in at the fake
cakes and fruit come mornings.

all this, typical for small town scandals and men of god.

come august,
all that was left of him were slippers
and a bible,
and, of course, what part of him
he left in the wombs of the elders' daughters.

last anyone heard, the deputy
found his clothes out by the rails,
cut all to hell.

one of the elders says
they saw a red beast pulling him into the sand.

and one of the believers says
the clouds parted and god brought him
home in a chariot of gold, salt, and fire.

but like most followers, people eye the ghost
woods out at the edge of town and the sheriff
writes the preacher's name on the list,
because that's what happens when people vanish.

every night when people get to the talking,
the drunk says one of the fathers put a couple
rounds in his belly and left him naked
at the bottom of the quarry
over near the fingertips of town.

                    *

when the mayor wants answers,
real answers, the sheriff lifts
the preacher's name from the list
and all his deputies spread out
like an armful of geriatrics
with metal detectors, or the slow
creep of sickness through
a village. they round up the usual
suspects for questioning.
at the station, there are cut lips and bruises
swelling up under
eyes and accusations.

                this is part of what gets said:

                            EXIT STAGE LEFT

ENTER STAGE LEFT – SOME USUAL SUSPECTS

when the guilty boys pass through the arbors
and valley rain,

it's like the dusting off of grandfathers'
guns or the cutting
out of lovers' tongues.
each flick of the wrist
howls at the slice
in family attics.

all of this, hardly
for convenience, but for something
tugging at the place below
their gut when the night gets heavy.

the old woman at the other side says,
"you young men should cover your tracks."

they had, though not in attics,
but the bottom of the quarry.

*

that night, it wasn't them who drove out
and stripped off
their clothes, wiped blood from their hands
and faces, and took turns
throwing what they could towards the center.

by morning, they were back
in their beds, and the sheriff had started
knocking on doors
for other reasons.

on the fifth front porch,
the middle daughter knows about trucks,
pissed off boys trying
to prove some points, and talk of a plan.

she wouldn't give names,
but said she heard voices leaking
through the vents in the bathroom.

these ones never had reason to do what they did,
they took a life simply 'cause it was there
to take and they didn't like it…

the body isn't found for years,
when the troopers try to pull
a truck from the reservoir and find what they let plunge.

by then everyone's gone to wherever they went.

EXIT STAGE RIGHT

dear sisters,

this town is killing me with all its gray and rain sputter. keeps me up nights. i miss the punch clock misery from my twenties.

when the rain really gets going here, i miss the dust and heat of our high desert, and the way lightning stretched itself across the horizon in summer as if it had the need to tear itself from the clouds, and what rain came only changed the smell of the place.

here, there's a constant smell of bark and swamp water, and, if i'm lucky, pine. though every now and again i smell oranges and charcoal leaking out of certain places.

there's constant misted-rain and everything's green, sprouting moss and ferns. on a map, this place is probably just a green square. and in the outskirts, everything is hills, slanting and rising, though this town is rectangular and boxed. when i walk through the cedar and pines, the moon gets massive, bloated, and lights most of town. it can't light the meadow behind the church, but when i walk it, the night lightens. though it's beautiful here, i'm craving the way the skyline looks with steel and glass at sunset.

the train whistles carry and echo from miles away into my window when it comes.

that's usually when the locals start locking their doors and windows, though i've seen no evidence of darker things.

OFFSTAGE – THE KILLING OF THOMAS HANSEN BY KATHRYN HANSEN

no. 41

no. 42

sometimes, stories can start like a coughful of smoke and the setting
of a scene. in this one, three broken bones brought this to blood,
and it started as she lied in bed tonguing the stitches her man put
on her lips.

> when the night undressed itself, stark naked and
> waiting

for the slow leak of dawn and railroad clatter that comes early
morning, she unsheaths the knife and waits for the first whistle.
when it sounds, she cuts across his throat

> like drawing a line between two points on a map.

her boy kept asking about his dad, the simple boyish kind of
questions kids ask when they wait, but she didn't tell him about
the shallow grave under the house, covered in lime and a couple
handfuls of cinnamon sticks. she simply looked

> her son in the eye, and said, "he's visiting a friend
> outta town." but his name made the list.

it's not the smell that gives her up, but the bloody sheets her
neighbor's mutt brings home on a sunday afternoon. a month later,
the cops pull her son from her like boards from a fence.

> that's when something snaps.

when she's watching her son drive away in the back seat of a cop
car. first it boils, then cuts loose and slides out. she shakes and
jitters, and starts

> growling at the topsoil and scratching
> at the lawn.

the end of this story's got funeral processions and closed caskets, jail bars and a boy who forgets all the bad things about his father,

all the good things about his mother.

so when the trial starts, he comes across town and fires his father's
pistol through the front window of the courtyard and got the bad
end of a couple bullets. when the smoke clears the bystanders

hear funeral jazz coming up from the rusted side
of town.

KATHRYN HANSEN'S DREAM SEQUENCE

at first, they thought it was the plague, said it was only
        a matter of time till
we were all bodies in a pile outside our own front doors.

but all i smell are oranges and charcoal. people stood on
        their porches for better views,
as if a crowd of eavesdroppers could cure just by listening or
        watching

the scenes unfold. but i fled, quick and quiet like a fox
        stealing apples from the prison
yard and they followed as voices usually do—

just marionettes gone free, shaking and rattling
        around upstairs whenever
a memory gets triggered or brought up.

these things are not things we lost in the fire,
        not the leftovers
of post-teen angst, or the hush of harbors at twilight.

        this is heavy and sudden like catching an anchor in
        the chest.

   *

        is that laughter or coughing coming from the tree
        line?

maybe it's just a coyote lurking in the brush 'cause here,
        secrets are damp,
caught in the space between the throat and the front teeth—

they only let 'em go when the time calls for it and someone
        important is listening...

no, it's kasey, and she hasn't had a holiday in ages, years maybe.
        today she's waiting in hospitals, the burn ward,
a thick smile sliding out from under her hood like a slit of sunlight

through a key hole as if she knows we will burn, and burn soon.

a train moans six blocks over and i'm hiding behind a stop sign,
       but something calls me inside—
something like an arpeggio in the key of d, dissected and put back
       together,

then fed back into itself—by the time the doors shut behind me, it's
       too late.
i'm staring at her. as she takes me by the arm, she keeps saying,

       "this is the undanced cadence of vanishing."

dear sisters,

this place feels as though it's breathing or whispering things about itself, and every day something new slips out from top window sills or out from half-open doors and finds its way to me. last week, i started writing these down. there's quite a collection: the sound of the wind coming from the mill, the smell of maple syrup and pine after thunder showers, the way some places smell of oranges and charcoal, or even the way birds circle the courthouse in afternoons. yesterday, whimpers from some melody came crawling from the alley. it stuck with me all day, and while i couldn't quite place each note, i muttered its words, "when i learn to sing, it'll change the key of everything."

the biggest thing is what everyone calls the vanishings. people just disappear.

sometimes, i can see groups gathered outside the sheriff's office, watching through the window when he writes a new name.

here, people learn that the vanishings belong to the ghost woods.

ENTER STAGE RIGHT – THE SHERIFF FINDS A TRAIL

past the downlands,
where everything tastes like salt
and limestone,
he touches the earth
as though it's the flesh of another's wife.
at contact,
hymns begin to swell in his head
and he can see the pews,
heads bowing,
and the preacher shouting,
"we are a hungry generation!"
this is where he finds the trail—
evidence of the flee.

he's not fond of the preacher, never was.
but he's a god-fearing man
and this search is his job.

it's the letter tacked to the list in his office
that sent him out. the writer had theories
about what happened to the preacher
and who was involved.

towns come and go, and he likes the way
landscapes tumble and roll.
up ahead,
footsteps carry like shouting voices.
the valley turns what noise makes its way inside
into heavy swings of sound.

EXIT STAGE LEFT

CUE BACKDROP – WHAT KIDS CALL THE GHOST WOODS

the ghost woods first showed themselves
in autumn after the first vanishing, when
the loggers started cutting their way and
found shallow graves. the sheriff, then
barely two weeks in, came back with
the men to find only a wall of trees,
no graves, no work done, and a pair of
sandals that belonged to the girl who had
vanished just days before. it didn't smell
of oranges and charcoal—never has—but
of swamp water and wet cedar. kids say
the trees uprooted themselves, plucked
the bodies from the ground, and cleaned
the scene. now, people say all that's there
are walking skeletons and ghosts with all
their ghost hair getting stuck in branches
and collecting in holes, their ghost voices
howling like wolves, breathing like rakes
scraping their way across the highway.

that afternoon, he went back to his office
and wrote her name on a list. years later,
he would write GHOST WOODS across
the top—not that he believed it, but the
town did, and he didn't want to rule out
anything. the list's been keeping him
busy, unmarried, but never lonely. he's
got each name and each life to keep him
entertained—he likes to imagine their
lives unfolding, picturing what led them
to the ghost woods. though, nothing
could explain that type of wandering.
and as the names gather on paper, on his
wall, he can't imagine scenarios, and this
lack wobbles around like a loose tooth for
years.

dear sisters,

for some reason, a parade of ghosts pass my bed after midnight, after the wolves have howled, and the crickets have forgotten what silence sounds like. they don't look at me or stop or even haunt my place. they just walk through walls as if they have places to be.

see, ghosts are quiet. no footsteps, no breathing, no voices, just the sound of a piano ringing out—that sound before it quiets, before a foot leaves the pedal. i slept through it for a week, just chalking it up to house noises. but tonight, i smell oranges and charcoal, and hear the sound again. i turn over, and there they are marching through, eyes heavy, steps slacked and graceful.

at first, my skin turns cold and my body moves itself back against the wall, hands rise like shields, fists in balls, but the ghosts keep on, don't notice me.

they aren't transparent or white, but dusty gray and dull, more like empty bodies coasting through walls.

i follow them.

once outside the house they separate. some go to houses, some towards the trees, or the church, or shop attics. i watch them through windows and over fences. they hover over sleeping bodies, watching.

CUE MUSIC – THE CHORUS

he's at it again, singing his story
under the street lamp outside the courthouse,
pausing on the good parts, to slow,
to let sink, and the chorus comes,

> "if i learn to sing, it'll change
> the key of everything."

though he's young with smooth
skin and well-kept clothes,
no marks of war
left on his body,
the smell of french cologne
and rosemary, it's no
secret that he is the town's
drunk, his inked fingers always zagging
through the air, conducting,
and what started
as maybe the follies of a young man
sewing oats and burning candles
is now clearly a man on his last
leg, hacking and wheezing
between notes, and every couple
hours one of the deputies pulls up
to send him on his way.

it's just habit by now,
'cause he'll wander back
half-tuned and spilling
every detail he can dig
up from "the good part
of his story," his teens and early
twenties, before the coda—
those stories—
the kind other drunks
from the city and other
towns tell, when his hands
would find her silhouetted
curves in the window-light,

when the paychecks bought decorations
and evenings out, before
he had wandered from the station
to town and stayed,
when his body hadn't been peeled
oranges, stripped down.

he huddles and shakes like toothaches,
and no longer sings in colder seasons.
years back winter was his favorite time,
the air chipped at his throat
and he'd spout a melody,
sing himself through the snow
and rain, the melody
working men and women and children
brought home with them.
families became choirs ringing
out inside homes,

> "when i learn to sing, it'll change
> the key of everything."

before the preacher came with his tent
revivals, organ chords, and acapella,
sermons, and salvation wrapped
up in the palm of his hands, these songs
meant something more than what they have become,
just fragments of words
and songs carved into the brick
wall of history by younger generations.

now this man is a fixture unkempt and dated
and out of tune like loose strings on a fiddle,
just noise drowning out the sound of water
and birds and town-shuffle.

when the air smells of salt
and pine and the lower tides,
he's here, trying again, recalling
his past word by word,

humming that melody,
vibrato and pitch trembling what's left
when each quits, chewing at the mouth
of whatever bottle he can find, and going on,

> "if i learned to sing, it would've changed
> the key of everything."

MUSIC CRESCENDOS

ENTER STAGE LEFT – THE SHERIFF FOLLOWS ANOTHER TRAIL

though the preacher's trail
turned ether, all the names on the list
had trails.
some dead ends.
some ended in the back of mills
or the overhangs of train stations
forty miles north, but some kept winding.

sometimes there are men, sometimes
women, but always a hasty grave,
shallow and half-covered in dried
ferns and strips of moss in the borders of town,
where the wolves roam when night drapes.

most bar-folk feel the itch to spit
rumors, but there are too many versions
stapling the walls. the sheriff
gets his leads because living in this town
taught him to filter.

today, he came back with a woman
whose name made the list. she's glacial,
her lips unmoving, her eyes pointed.
when the deputies come to see her,
they ask the sheriff why the cell
smells of oranges and charcoal.

EXIT STAGE RIGHT

SPOTLIGHT UPSTAGE RIGHT – IN A NEW TOWN

after the trigger-pulls, the guilty boys
didn't catch the train.
they took their father's truck and chased
the logging roads,
till they found the highway
tracing the bay.

see, their names were written
on the list two days before the preacher's.
though, that was their plan. the week before,
they filled the bar with boasting.
they would best the ghost woods.

on sunday night, they followed the preacher
out to the orchard.

now, in the next town,
small enough to learn and large enough to stay
unnoticed, they found a motel
tucked near the lungs of the town,
where visitors hardly went, and locals
found themselves every sunday
when church was done and dinner waited.

at night, the boys drank in bars and read
headlines for news from home.

one stayed quiet and to himself,

the other made friends.
found his bed later and later, till morning would beat
him back to the motel, and the other
woke alone in the curtain-light.

STAGE LIGHTS UP

dear sisters,

i was on the bar stool, nursing a maker's mark when the voice and the choral echo climbed in through the windows. the "amen," the applause, the hollering, lifted me from my seat, carried me through the doors, led by my chest, these sounds tugging at my ribcage.

outside, i saw the glow from inside the church at the far shoulder of town, heard a voice say, "we've been blessed by the lord, we've been given a house of worship, a place to exalt that is sturdy and made of brick and stone to keep our praises safe..." the front doors open and the congregation sings, "our god is an awesome god," letting it filter into the street for the non-believers to witness.

and i'm pulled right into that church and up to the altar, coasting.

the preacher touched my forehead with his palm and it burned though my body and turned my lower half to water. i tumbled back, the spirit in me, shuffling around, scraping what it could against my insides, down my throat into my lungs and belly, and falling into my legs and feet, burrowing, pumping.

ENTER STAGE LEFT – THE SHERIFF QUESTIONS THE CITY SHARKS

in their warehouses of dank air and moisture,
and casinos popping with shuffling,
chatter, and tobacco smoke, they only
laugh when they hear about the preacher—
they collected weeks ago, maybe months.

they know of no other debts or city-trouble,
said the preacher's been absent since
paying up.

*

empty-handed, he catches another trail
pushing down the coast and finds a woman,
number 58 on the list, her face
contracts when he stands in front of her.

she tries to turn, but he clutches
her arm and cuffs it to his,
says her name, and pulls her along.

she gives it up, lets it slack, and by mid-day
number 59's crossed out and the town-talk
quickens, but there's no trial.

he finds her body unmoving in the cell,
gray, barely warm.

EXIT STAGE LEFT

CUE BACKDROP – THE CHURCH GETS A NEW ELDER

on a sunday night, the train came,
heaving as it passed through, stopping
only to let a man off. his body, thin and
fragile. he walked like an old man.

the preacher met him on the platform,
brought him in, told people this was his
kid-brother, though the preacher looked
younger, and they looked nothing alike.

they ate in the kitchen, turntable playing
jazz, conversations about things followers
would only wince at.

the next sunday, introductions were made
and he spoke.

"god has brought me here to be with you.
i was headed south when i felt a tugging
at my chest, it yanked and yanked. so, i
came west. i do not know my reason for
being here, but i have faith that god will
show us together."

the congregation nodded as they're
supposed to, hands folded, waiting for
worship, the prayer, the sermon.

dear sisters,

i know i spent all those sundays embarrassed by your theatrics, by father's knack for making scenes when worship began. i should've been used to it, but till i left, i was ashamed. you all would flail, tumble through the aisle, spit tongues like curses, and swear it was god's voice, swear that god's fire had found its way into your limbs. and after service, dad too exhausted to eat.

i only started raising my hands to avoid judgment. not for god, but for the churchgoers, and it became habit. but now, god's fire is sifting in me, constantly boring deeper, constantly speaking during service.

this is an apology. i'm sorry i thought it was an act.

OFFSTAGE – THE KILLING OF DICKY GREEN BY SAMANTHA GREEN

blindsided by her appearance at the diner's window, he looks from her glare to his eggs, watches them cool and waits for her to leave, but like always, her presence stays, clawing its nails into his side.

she starts tapping the window

when he doesn't look back, slow and steady quarter notes till he looks again, and she points with one-handed jabs. she probably would've stayed for hours.

she likes to put fear in him. it makes her

stomach turn and her knees shake with pleasure, but one of the sheriff's deputies saw her there, heard the tapping, and left his place at the counter to send her along.

he doesn't know the details of how they met in the garden behind the church, both pulling weeds for money, or how the wedding in the church stayed small and quiet, and the preacher pronounced their names wrong, or the honeymoon in their own apartment above the grocery store. he knows the later stories, knows about the wounded walls in their old home like pock marks, the bruises on bodies like water color spreading across paper, the screaming, the divorce, the scene in court with the bailiff and blood and "fucks."

he knows the poor boy just tries to keep his distance, but she keeps finding him.

the deputy comes over and puts his hand on his shoulder, asks, "you ok?" he doesn't look up,

just shrugs the hand off and says, "no."

*

months later, when the town catches
whiffs of charcoal and oranges peeling,
and some people say the ghost woods
are at work, these two names make the list
but the sheriff finds her trail two towns over,
headed towards the eastern cities.

SAMANTHA GREEN'S DREAM SEQUENCE

there's a slick rumble lathering through my chest, and when it
      settles, the house is quiet.
the party broke hours ago, and all my friends left debris

in rows from room to room, so cleaning is easy. and as i gather
      the trash and bag it,
i catch the smell of oranges and charcoal lifting from the floor.

in the back room, the floor has been swept and cleaned, and all
      that's left is a girl in the shaded
corner of the room. she's staring out a big window and tapping
      a steady beat on the glass.

                i hear a piano ringing out from

behind her, notes lifting, as though her breaths have
      let them into the room.
i get real close, but can't see her eyes. i know she's here for me.
      the room seizes and buckles
when she looks at me and says, "can you hear that cadence?

it's yours. it belongs to you and what you've done. wait. listen."
      and she rises, but i do not watch her.

                the piano scales into the higher notes till it
                clicks out steady quarter-notes without tune.

ENTER STAGE RIGHT – THE BROTHER

the preacher's brother takes the reigns,
starts preaching when the followers
allow it—they need the word delivered.

his body moves differently, voice slower,
and his messages aren't the same.
he takes his time to make his points,
doesn't stomp the ground or slap at the air.

he simply speaks as though each word came from stone.

he points to the ceiling
only when he says, "the lord."

he does not muster his sermons with fear.
he does not scream the devil's name, but whispers it,
says it slowly, so that they remember it as something
quiet and methodical.

                    *

when asked about his brother, he does not
shed or crumble,
he only shakes his head
and tightens his lips.

"may the lord be with him."

during his first service, he tells stories,
one by one,
about kentucky and that old coming of age where
wheat is something you run your fingers
through, where magic hours
turn honest men to liars, where boys
cut their teeth on learning
what the bible says
and what it meant to live by it.

the congregation applauds

and believes he is speaking about others.

EXIT STAGE RIGHT

dear sisters,

the church isn't fancy, but it's clean and worked-in like a good baseball glove. even the pews have pockets from where followers-past sat before they vanished or left. i've taken a spot in the back where a young couple sat till early fall. they say their names—and others—during prayer, so it goes long.

the congregation has come to know me not by name, but by where i am during service. we are not a rowdy church, not like back home. we always sing, and sometimes, we shout "amen" or applaud, but the preacher's always going, always half-fire and suffering in the heat of late mornings. his eyes never resting, constantly flicking through all of us as he gives us our bread and warnings.

OFFSTAGE – THE KILLING OF EMILY NORTHRUP BY OLIVER NORTHRUP

no. 27
no. 28

after the affair had run its course, the places they met grew
heartbeats and singing voices. these places crooned, told him stories
and sometimes they'd snicker at him, when he passed on his way to
work.

> those places carried secrets calling
> names and false shores.

every night, he let his pickup idle and he'd stare in through the
windows of these places just to feel his gut turn and hear
the wind play songs from ohio. when morning split out across
buildings, he knew he was nothing more than a one-man

> carnival of mama's boys and glass jaws.

he tries and tries to let the guilt slip from him like cutting an
anchor loose. he keeps saying, now that he's in her shadow, "cool it
with the history."

> but night is a trapdoor in a bedroom.

the guilty ones—depending on their motives, how much time
passed since the incident, or how long guilt is willing to trudge
itself along and follow—usually end up trying to shake off
nightmares from the night before.

> but some don't, some sleep like the
> dead from the southwest.

those are the ones who did not act in passion, the ones who
hatched plans and followed through.

> they'll get what they get when the gates
> call their names.

the others, the ones with passion, can't always remember the

125

dreams, 'cause they don't always stick, but the feeling does. it spreads, crawling from the skin, into the mouth, down the throat, to settle inside the stomach,

to burn, to wait.

this man hid north of the lake in the east corner of the state—went straight there after he fired six bullets and left the house on market street. still, with all the quiet, the space, and the smell of pine and cedar, he can't find a night's sleep without the same dream.

these he remembers, though
they're not nightmares,

they're different, darker than dreams, warnings maybe, or prophecies, calling to him, telling him something approaches for him.

it usually happens something like this:

OLIVER NORTHRUP'S DREAM SEQUENCE

in the window-light, i sit and wait for the undanced cadence
      of vanishing, for that thick
silence milking over my skin. growing every hour, my body
      collecting

          fat as if it was catching lint.

outside, the suffering moves and breathes, kicking up dust and
spores smelling of charcoal and oranges. trekking through town
towards the pass in search of better light, advanced medicine, and
free plots

of land to make their own. passing through, we converse
      about those things
and the fires witnessed weeks back, when the counterfeiters
      from denton
congregated around the sewer drain outside the post office
      demanding something
real to crucify. we handed them a bag of love letters, but they did
      not read, they did not open
a single letter, or even hold it up to the sunlight, to steal a glance
      of its contents.
they formed a circle, heaved the bag, and set the burlap and paper
      to fire, singing,
"don't trust the suits they're all in cahoots with the evil one."
      and in the window-light,
i sit, still waiting, and the conversations have vanished
      with the suffering,
and now, kasey stands in the doorway with her hood up, like
      always, and she's nodding,
as she pours gasoline all over the walls, all over the floor, all over
      the man
in the window-light, and she smiles as she strikes a match.

          this is how the room is set on fire.
          this is how it burns.

dear sisters,

have i told you about the ghost woods? i must have.

lately they've been slipping into sermons, and today, the preacher went straight at it, saying, "they hold no mystery. you believers know many from our flock, from our neighborhoods who've disappeared among those branches. that's not mystery, that's the devil's draw. unheard unless you really listen. so listen to the sound of the devil's red mouth call like a hi-hat through a verse. repent your sins and god will tune your ears to know that putrid sound."

though i can see them from my window, i've never been, never heard the call.

so tonight, i went to the edge of the ghost woods to cross the threshold. i never saw ghosts breaching the tree line, but i believed that this was their source. when i got to its reaches, branches practically petting my face, i couldn't go on. something tugged at the back of my ribcage, away from the woods.

i sat on the half-standing wall of boulders and stared into the depths. i heard things moving inside, just beyond sight, where the dark curls into shapes and spaces. could've been ghosts, or wolves hunting, or trees making plans.

then i heard the piano noise coming down from the mill.

ENTER STAGE LEFT – THE GHOST WOODS, THE DARE

a girl took the dare and, in august,
wandered in just to prove
that there were no ghosts
in the woods,
but once she breached
the tree line, dark came.
when she turned around her path was gone.

the trees had lifted
themselves from the ground
and thickened.
it was dark, but light
enough to see the skeletons,
shallow graves, scraps of clothing and human things
like parts of tents, rusted pots and pans and forks,
saddles, sleeves of clothing, all of this,
left in what could've been
a retreat or a scattering attempt to find a way out.

days after the girl went in, the trees
parted at night, let her
out into the orchard.
the sound of voices carried her
down the rows.
she heard them retreating,
a gravel crunching,
and then she smelled blood.

EXIT STAGE LEFT

ENTER STAGE RIGHT – THERE'S BLOOD IN THE ORCHARD, BUT NO BODY

in the spider light of an orchard, a girl found dirt and blood in rows,
       bruised into the ground.
she moves to stay warm and alert among the shadows, shivers
       'cause this dark cold
sticks to the body, gathers and tugs little flocks of night like cattle
       at the spark of winter.
and siren light clears the shadow back to where it came from,
       and all that color wakes her
from her stupor and shaking, to recall and retell what's been done.

LIGHTS FADE TO DARKNESS

SPOTLIGHT CENTER STAGE – THE SMELL

the smell has always been here, the town only thought it was
coming from river water and mud,

       but

when it started
pouring up
from the quarry,
from under houses,
some boys started
asking old-
timers if it always
smelled like this.

       the answer spread

through the followers, then the town, pushing itself, squeezing
through open window
cracks, and slow shutting doors.

when bodies showed, the smell thickened
and wandered through the meat of town, staging
itself in clothes, hovering above standing water,
and as bodies turned up, the smell began to settle
at the entrances of alleys and the backside of buildings.

STAGE LIGHTS UP

CUE BACKDROP – BROTHERS AND SISTERS

each sister's belly held babies,
"bastards," the followers
called them
and so parents sent them
away,
forgot them. the followers
laughed
at these teenaged accusations,
at the lazy finger pointing to a
man of god.
these boys, these brothers,
they believed as brothers
should.

but here, it doesn't matter
what you believe,
what you know,

it only matters what is said
from the pulpit.

dear sisters,

i can't say i believe everything coming from the preacher's lips. some of it sounds too heavy and comes out sloppy, spitting out of his mouth when he gets going for real, rambling about god's love and sin's grip on man.

he does look convincing, sounds convincing, as if everything that comes from him comes from god. he's never really behind the pulpit for more than a second or two to grab the proper reading of a verse or find his place in his sermon. instead he likes to carry himself up and down the aisles and in front of the stage. one time he screamed, "god will protect you if you let him! banish sin from your door, peel its grip from your body parts!" and slammed the piano keys four times. their echo hovered above the congregation for minutes before he spoke again.

sometimes, he likes touching arms and shoulders and foreheads if the moment calls for it. sometimes, he likes to sing certain verses from song of solomon or leviticus in quarter notes and he moves as though each part of his body are the gears inside of a clock, constantly pushing time forward, circling. i can feel the spirit, even when i doubt. it burns in my throat, and my ribcage tugs when he speaks. i shout things like "amen" and "preach on brother."

it's clear the spirit's in others too, though they seem to believe everything that's said. it's the way their eyes gloss over the longer he speaks.

inside glows with all its candle and sky-light, the organ's behind the pulpit, next to the piano, and all the gold veining its way through the heart of the ceiling, down into the cross against the front wall. our voices rise and scale the brick walls and up to the ceiling, coating them before it quiets, and up comes the smell of brick and copper, with the occasional hint of citrus and coal mines.

if i didn't know any better, i'd call it lust i see in the followers, they practically sweat it from their pores. they don't lick their lips or bat their eyelashes, but blush when he speaks, eyes watering when he comes close. after church they speak to each other as though the other wasn't there, as though the sermon was spoken from the closet, inside a bedroom, at daybreak.

OFFSTAGE – THE KILLING OF RUTH COLLINS BY RUSSELL LEE

no. 20

no. 21

there are crimes and there are crimes of passion. if someone found
him right afterwards, he'd probably say

> it was neither, but a necessity born
> out of shame.

today, he'd tell you otherwise, and he tries to scrape it from his past
like bark from a tree, but it's tied to his ribcage and only tightens
when he tries to free it.

> the night it went down, he entered
> though the back,

put a burlap bag over his head, and stood over the bed—once
theirs—and used a pillow to muffle the shots.

> instead of shooting, he used the pillow
> to snuff her out.

took three hours of sitting inside his car, three blocks down, across
the ball park, loading and unloading shells into the chamber of his
pistol. walking through how it would go.

> when it was over, he remembered

how she'd lay herself on their living room floor, fold her arms across
her chest and say,

> "this is what i'd look like in a casket…"

> and

> "am i still pretty when i'm dead?"

people fall in love in the key of c and out of it with dissonance, climbing its way into a scale.

that night, he made her bed, cleaned the house, carried her from the house to his car, and left her body a mile from the quarry in the place kids call the ghost woods.

he tells bartenders about his dreams, the ones starting afterwards, about kasey always clicking the chamber of his pistol and saying,

"what i do and what i should are like brothers."

*

her name was number 20 on the list. today the sheriff's found parts of her body under a stump. one of the deputies says, "who's that?"

the sheriff straightens up and pulls the list from his shirt pocket. he unfolds it and reads her name as though he's never read it before.

sometimes, songs begin, almost like this:

RUSSELL LEE'S DREAM SEQUENCE

it's not a helicopter scaling its way down the side of the building.
        this begins from train windows
watching willows lit by moon-ricochet in the thick pitch—

someone says, "night hums when the moon's out," and sometimes
        if it's just right
you can see faces ghosted up in burlap, ready for robberies.

they'll show at the edge of tracks, moving towards the wreck,
        barrels slitting through
the damp mist of the hillside. now, from train windows i see kasey.

kasey and her black hood floating towards me, like a stalled truck
        through an intersection
as if the moon is guiding her. the train, even slower,
        and when i touch

my face, there's blood. only it's gray and thin as water.
        when the door swings up
kasey's there, smirking like a crowbar lodged
        underneath a deadbolt

        someone says, "this cadence will be danced."

she's holding my shoulders, when the train stops at the bluff, its
        cliffs tumbling down
into where the pacific had laid itself. it's not salt i taste in the air

        but skin, worse yet, the skin of my wife.

wolves howling sound like footsteps
in grass or leaves plucking themselves
from branches, as if there's nothing else to do.

kasey says, "down there's where boys get covered
in dirt, boys become men overnight, they learn to earn
their keep for comebacks, second chances,
and the opening and closing of gates."

CURTAIN FALLS

dear sisters,

i woke this sunday exiting the house. this is the work of the spirit. i backslid into drinking and bent into the early morning, but that morning, my body had lifted and dragged me from bed, still drunk. i tried to retreat back into my covers, but my ribcage became the needle of a compass pointing towards the church, and my legs dragged through the alley and out into the street, and through the front doors, into my place in the pews.

ACT II – CURTAIN RISES REVEALING THE PLACE OF LIGHT AND SHADOW

a newcomer wakes in the place of light and shadow.

SPOTLIGHT FOLLOWS THE ACTION

1.

history is kept this way

2.

i am not the only one here in this light and shadow.

bodies stand in what light gets through to strengthen
their shadow.

word is, the stronger the shadow the better the chances
to visit above.

here, the sky is a river and many of us stand in place
looking up.

the air tastes like oranges and charcoal, smells like wet fur
and wheat fields at magic hour.

the silence in here sounds like a grand piano
echoing in a hall.

expecting to wake at the bottom of the quarry, i became
speechless

there, watching all the bodies move around through
all the dark spots,

speaking to each other about how they got here,
starting with, "i woke…"

thing is, most of us know each other from town,
faces are all we get.

all that's left to do is catch up and clarify what went down.

we know who put us here. most of us saw it happen.
the trigger, the knife, the blunt swing.

i saw two boys, followers, approaching the orchard's toes.
saw a couple sparks flare in the dark,

and felt a searing trail inside my chest. i went black before i could
see their faces, but i knew who they were.

3.

every town's got a place like this with all the bodies underneath.
only some ceilings aren't like ours.

some are made of rock, or corn stalks, or sand, or ice. but it's the
same, everyone likes to stare up at it.

this is kasey's place, but above, we believed this was the ghost
woods. most of us here only make half of the list.

4.

could be months pass before i see her,

      kasey.

only her hood's down, hair's up, and she's not smiling—tight-lipped
and head shaking as she approaches.

i ask if she's god.

"no and this ain't heaven—with all the lies you told up there, be
glad it ain't. you'd be kept out for sure, but our gates were always
open for you. we were waiting."

when she touches me, i understand that this could be worse,
that here is not hell, that here is not heaven, but here is my home.

5.

according to the rest of the bodies, kasey occupied everyone's
dreams, but doesn't choose, selection breathes

on its own. i had heard others telling the same stories. what's she
doing up there, i couldn't tell you, but the big

body with the shadow thick as pitch says kasey's patrolling for the
guilty ones, the ones who put us here.

everyone laughs at him, says we're the ones not in heaven, the ones
ghosting our families at night, that we're the guilty ones.

but the thick-shadowed body says he's seen
them come in, seen them dragged into the far end of here,

where there's dust-light, past the older bodies. says, "we are the
victims." says, "there is a place for the guilty ones kasey's captured."

6.

we make fires out of water and watch it stream from the floor to
our ceiling. god how all we want is new bodies, real ones.

this is where i learn of all the visits.

we are allowed out together, single file, to rise at the center of town.
kasey does not watch us,

but i stay on path at first. there are no oranges and charcoal
when we're out.

that's how i know she's away, that's when i learn to stray.

7.

no one guards the door.

kasey's constantly mocking the ones with shadows like gauze,
craning her neck at the water above.

they don't stand a chance, but no one really tries to leave forever. we
are supposed to only leave for a few looks here and there.

it's as though kasey wants to see who has the guts to haunt in the
day. the one with the shadow

thick as pitch has a chance, but he won't go near the door before
night falls. he stares at the door,

watches for dark. when we're out, he wanders over to the diner and
stares in the window.

sometimes, he wanders around
behind the buildings.

i heard one got out, but returned probably days later, ashamed: his
family sent him away.

8.

days i stood under the light, moving with it as needed.

now, i leave letters for my brother.

my shadow widens, darkens, but i don't dare leave when we're not allowed.

kasey's presence tends to be thicker near the door when the sun's still out.

it's humid and weighted, even when she's not seen for months.

i'm afraid to see her in town.

what she would do.

but when the rest of us line up, i keep wandering from the group.

9.

i don't believe the letters i leave ever get read,
but i know why.

to find them is a task itself. i leave these letters
on the backs

of stop signs, in bark, on the face of rocks,
on garage floors.

if people see this, they'll think some kids
are running wild, playing ghosts.

see, i cannot write in words, just the vertical lines.
the reader

must cross with horizontal lines to make
words.

i'm not sure if my brother's even noticed them, but
if he saw them,

i would like to think he'd know they're mine.

10.

so, we visit, watch our past pass us by, watch everyone age.

back down there, we talk of our visits.

sometimes, we gather at the foot of our old beds and watch
our wives and husbands or lovers with new men and women.

we envy not the act, jealous not of the sex, but of the bodies,
still alive.

we can never find the ones who put us here. most new bodies
start with that search,

but give up for visiting families.

a girl keeps talking about her killer, and one night she finds him,
sprawled in the river, gray.

she watches him, and by morning the current's carried him through
the canyon and into the quarry.

someone wonders why she's the only one who's
ever seen her killer.

the one with the shadow says they've all been captured.

i am not interested in that kind of search.
what could be done anyway?

i haven't seen them once since i've been going up.

11.

someone opens their gray mouth, says, "these children will not know their fathers."

to some, it eats at their skin and softens their eyes.

to some, it quiets.

to some, it leads them to pockets of light, and though they thicken their shadows, they do not rise when it's not allowed.

12.

a new one falls from the ceiling. the man used to live down the
street from me, but i cannot say his name.

he wakes as though he had been sleeping. he does not know who put
him here, but days later his son falls down,

holding the air like he's clenching a gun. he tells him who it was.

13.

14.

history is made differently above.
or at least the outcomes are different.

above, history tells us the ghost woods claimed us, but we know
now that is just a bundle of trees with stories tacked to it.

one body asks kasey if she owns the ghost woods.

kasey laughs, says, "the ghost woods do what they need. they don't
belong to anyone."

every body that falls here adds to its claim.

all of us have our names on the list in the sheriff's office—

so are the names of the ones who put us here.

15.

the wind comes, keeps cutting at our bodies, shakes us,
pushes against

our outsides like the weight of another, pressing down come
morning.

the wind comes when kasey's been gone for stretches.
that orange and charcoal

taste fills our mouths as though someone's shoved it through our
teeth.

when the wind settles, she appears, stalks through the center of us
without a word.

we wipe the taste the wind left on us, in us.

16.

talk of visits gets old,
and all we really do up there is watch.

it's clear my letters aren't being read.

we stand at bedsides, watching them stir in their sleep,
we stand in doorways, watching our children grow without us,
we stand at the tree line, watching our lovers love others,

      and it goes,

around the fire,

we share what we do up there around our families,
we elaborate, change our tone, wave our hands, clench our fists.

but the circle gets real tired of all that, of all that shame,
of all the if-i-could'ves and i-only-should'ves.

      conversation drifts

and the other bodies start talking
about the captured ones.

curiosity sends me after answers, down past
where the oldest bodies huddle waiting
for their shadows to thin and peel away,

      piece by piece.

when i pass,
they don't bother to look up,
they just hum melodies to songs from orchestras.

the place gets quiet,
sound leaves its place and dies as it lifts and shadows scatter
out and away from each other like fresh blood in water.

i step through,

clearing them away with my hands,
and there, at the end of a tunnel:

a hatch door.

i open it
counterclockwise till the door opens, swinging out
and inside, there are cells lining the wall,
and behind each bar there are human faces.

this is where they keep the guilty ones.

CURTAIN FALLS

ACT III – CURTAIN RISES REVEALING THE TOWN AT DUSK

the sheriff's out and the town's getting used to the new preacher.

SPOTLIGHT CENTER STAGE – THE SHERIFF'S MORNING MEETINGS

now, every morning he meets
his deputies at the back table in the diner,
where the late-nighters sip coffee,
smoke cigarettes, and slide
gossip back and forth across the table.

he wants updates, leads.

a few mornings ago, he assigned
each one trails, names to follow, and passed
out hand-written copies of the list,
half names, half xxs.

he said, "these are not vanishings anymore.
these are names of both
suspects and victims, disappearances and criminals."

the deputies don't eat breakfast at these meetings.
it's clear these young men let panic in to bump
around—

*

when the ghost woods owned the cause,
fear took a breath.

murder's taking claim means safety's
been unhitched and reset,
and these deputies will walk home
tonight with loose shoulders and quickened eyes.

STAGE LIGHTS UP

dear sisters,

the spirit left me today.

came up from my feet, through my lungs, and out my throat. i did not exorcise the spirit. this was not a choice. it left when i saw the preacher climbing through an elder's daughter's window. curiosity sent me to the sill, where i saw his hands all over her skin, his clothes on the floor, his hips to hers like husbands' and wives'.

i see her brothers at the corner of the block looking over, waiting for him to exit, speaking to each other like wolves at the tree line.

CUE BACKDROP – THE STATION

to find railroad tracks, you have to cut
east through the ankles of town and cross
the county line bridge, and even then the
train doesn't come through more than
twice a month, bringing goods, drifters,
and passers-by on their way north.

standing on the platform, it looks like all
there is in these parts is a station, trees,
halves of buildings, and steady rainfall
kicking at the ground.

if the train comes through when the night
bleeds into daylight, as though it's leaking
through cloth, you can hear wolves
ending their prowl, birds fading out, and
frogs singing in half notes.

the preacher once stood on this same
platform. but he saw something
prosperous in the bleak skyline, felt
something tug at his ribcage like a wire
connected to the sunrise.

could've been the smell of oranges and
charcoal that pleased him, but whatever
it was, he had visions, saw a congregation
to feed, stacked inside the brick of a
building, he felt the soft heat of candle
light and heard the organ swell and voices
gathered and spreading in praise, and saw
his hands spreading fire with the touch of
god.

the north no longer called his name, so he
took his things from the train and hiked
into where the town was huddled, in the
clearing a mile up from the canyon.

he set up a tent twenty paces from the
general store and every night
in the glow he'd ask his congregation,
"you like jazz in the city?" and no one
would answer, but some might squirm or
roll shoulders, and he'd go on,
"jazz tucks the devil between the scales
and stops, fixes things so you think what
you're hearin's got beauty in it, truth in
it, but all it's got is hell-fire and adultery,
bible-burnin' and sloth. if you put your
ear up to a git-tar, you can hear the
chanting of hell, 'we got you
where we want you,' over and over, till
you're fallin' with the rest."

and they followed his words 'cause he
spoke like he meant it, moved like a man
who knew how the world turned, dancing
his way through sermons, spit-firing verses
as though it would be the last breath he
ever gave.

dear sisters,

last night, i heard gunshots in the orchard and hours later i heard a girl scream. the sheriff's lights flashed till morning and all the deputies scoured the row. all i've heard is that there was a pool of blood, but no sign of a body.

ENTER STAGE RIGHT – THE SHERIFF KEEPS CROSSING OFF NAMES

the blame gets heavy against his back,
real lopsided and constant—
all those vanishings, all those names
let go to paper when
they could've been the clear end of a trail.

he remembers who they were before
they were just names.

the deputies keep saying, "no one expected this,"
fear trickling out with each word.
he expected—or
the wiser parts of his young body once did—
but he kept blindly adding to the list,
pages and pages,
'cause that's what was done.

       *

first ten times were the hardest,

on porches, watching knees buckle and the way
parents and spouses grasped for bracing,
wailing those uncontrollable moans,
guttural, expanding.

he tells his deputies, "we're rewriting their lives."

this part of the whole thing is taxing.
it quiets him.
lets him sleep only a couple hours at a time,
and when he does, he dreams
about new murders, new
bodies surfacing—every lump in a field
becomes a grave, every stump
hides a body.

       *

one deputy returns with a man—
number 147—found
east, in a cabin between here and the next town.

that suspect won't give up
whereabouts, but he's got all of his girl's
things under his cot,
and she's number 148.
"i ain't saying shit," he says.
by five, he's all
black-eyed and loose-toothed,
spitting blood on the floor with even less to say.

a week later, the deputies find her body
in the husk of brush in the far corner of the meadow
behind the church.

                    *

the sheriff knows this man and his girl,
saw them on several occasions in their lawn
battling out
jealousy and the wages of youthful engagements.

when morning meets the dark he's still up,
watching the bruises swell and the sun
pry itself out over the trees.
the smell of oranges and charcoal
plows into the cell-room, and he coughs,
the citrus and coal scrambling into his nose and throat.
the fit passes and he looks back to the man,
that body graying slowly.

he reports this to the mayor—
"every suspect grays during the night,
and now, i've witnessed it."
—the mayor puts his feet up and slurs,
"it's just the ghost woods coming to collect."

EXIT STAGE LEFT

dear sisters,

i've reclaimed my spot at the bar and the preacher's name made the list.

pulling at my glass of maker's, i heard a conversation in the corner of the room, where the light practically swayed from dim to dark and back again, it crept over to me as if i was supposed to be part of it, as though it kept tapping my shoulder saying, "join."

someone said, "that's three more."

someone else said, "when was the last time there were three?"

"years ago."

there was a storm that day, thunder smacking around like someone's pounding the glass of a neighbor's house, but the conversations carried in jitters and stopped only when the storm dragged itself inside the doors, where men shook the rain from their coats, from their hair.

the three they're talking about: the preacher, and two boys— one of the elder's sons.

OFFSTAGE – KASEY'S IN THE DREAMS OF BRUCE POWELL

no. 155
kasey

i stop at the borders of dreams and peer in like at a kitchen window,
hoping for a glimpse of the life inside.

      but i am not here to look. i am here to collect

what needs collecting. a common misconception among the
guilty ones is that these dreamscapes are mine. i don't paint these,
or hollow out the rocks for buildings, or even hang lights in the
basements. i just make use of them.

      and when there's a piano, i play it.

these dreamers follow me when i ask them to, and as i navigate, i
can feel them tremble behind, following when they don't have to,
complying 'cause they think all this is mine,

      or maybe it's guilt pulling them after me.

how i find them is easy, there's always an artifact of the crime—a
weapon, evidence, a location—hanging around the scene, noticed
or unnoticed among the actions,

      and so i find them in some kind of
      lighting that fits

the crime, and they look at me as though we've met, when we
haven't, and say my name as though they know it, when they don't,
and follow me, no real questions,

      into the edges of shadows.

there's no secret room carved in the back of a mountain where i tell
them their purpose. this is nothing more than me finding our way
out.

and sometimes, exits sound like this:

BRUCE POWELL'S DREAM SEQUENCE

the sun quivers in the heat, but my arms bump and tighten.
       i hear a piano somewhere over the ridge,
down where the sun can't catch a thing, and the wind comes
       through the valley carrying

the sounds of wagon trains and children. my body whips and
       buckles like a scorpion tail at the end
of a fight. i tumble back against the brick part of town,
       where the farmland

gives up its arms, the streets still, and moss covers where it can
       reach, and shiny things have not found
their way up towards the sky, they remain folded in the papers of
       architects.

       now, i can see her at the piano.

hood up, fingers poised, playing, then waiting, playing, then
       waiting.

       she must sense me. she straightens up,
       and lifts her foot from the pedal,
       and plays a series of minor chords,
       and when i'm close enough to touch her,
       she leans away

and starts playing a waltz, staccato and slow, but i think of winter
       and start shivering, i look at my feet,
at my bare feet, now covered in the water pouring from the top
       of the piano,

       and when i look up kasey's there,
       i can feel her breath on my skin,
       sticky, smelling of mandarin oranges
       and charcoal.

dear sisters,

i haven't seen the ghosts in a while, but now there are more bodies, and there's one here who's got more of a face than i've ever seen on these ghosts. its not just the flat mass of a head like the others. it's got holes where the eyes should be and a slit where the mouth is, vibrating as it parades through, and the start of cheekbones, smoothing out.

i've started following this one.

this became a nightly task. i'd sleep early, just to get up when they came. i'm still at it.

most of them just watch, but this new body never goes to the same place. he's always marking things on the back of signs, under seats, on the bottom of pews, on the corner of alley walls. i can see the messages at night, but they aren't words, just rows of lines. in mornings they look like faded chalk lines.

OFFSTAGE – THE KILLING OF KAVEH SMITH BY DAWN SMITH AND DOUGLAS MCGUIRE

no. 17

no. 18

no. 19

anyone can smell its musk from the other room, somewhere
between used linen and dead skin.

hear it, too.

it screams.

sometimes, it sings in the darkest parts of morning before the birds
start calling.

inside the room, bedside lamps keep half
of their faces hidden when they speak. one
touches the cuts under her eyes from accidents.

"oh fuck, think of all the murder i could bleed for you."

but it's too late. the smell follows them to work,
the sound wraps itself around the fabric of their clothes,
each piece of hair. it wakes them up every two hours.

"just this one time."

STAGE LIGHTS UP

THE SHERIFF'S DREAM SEQUENCE – THE GIRL

a gathering of followers surrounds the girl's body like a banquet
        of vultures on a hay
bale at noon. one by one they inch closer, and particles
        of rust and dirt

dance in the shaft of light pushing its way through the tree line,
        and when i
get closer to the backs of men and women around the body,

for some reason i think of his father, or the way
        my son strums d minors
on the porch after a day of plowing and pulling, crooning,

> "the night is still as if the night can
> forgive if it's warm and dark enough,
> but thing is, when there's blood in
> the air, the night does not forgive."

*

i push my way to the center and crouch as though i'm standing on
        a patch of ice. her body is gray,
her eyes closed. i smell oranges and charcoal.

the crowd's gasps collect and spew out above them in one four-part
        harmony,

> "the night is still as if the night can
> forgive if it's warm and dark enough,
> but thing is, when there's blood in
> the air, the night does not forgive."

this does not remind me of my father or son.

> this is brutal and clear and has
> capsized the hope of this girl's safe return.

CUE ALL LIGHTS

dear sisters,

some little girls and boys sing about the preacher. they made up songs.

"the preacher's in a hole in the center of the ghost woods, buried by the branches in the middle of the night. listen to his voice it has sneaked up to the mill, listen to his sermons still promising to heal."

i hear this song daily, lifting out from behind the school-house, from backyards.

i asked my boss about it. he said the foundation sunk and cracked. all the wind pushes through that space—it's the way they built the thing, all concrete and wood walls bending and warping with water and age. he said it's been doing that since he was a kid.

i've been up there when the wind hit. it came at me, swelling, building speed, and turned the corner, coming through as a choir crescendos through an opening door.

dear sisters,

i snuck into the sheriff's office last night and tacked a letter to the top of the list. it's bigger than i thought. it's pages of names, all tiny and handwritten. my letter wasn't a ton of proof. it wasn't even anything more than giving them something i witnessed right before the preacher died.

i'm not scared of the repercussions—they know i saw them. i met eyes with the smaller one and he just stayed there, not saying anything. it's been months since, but the girl who the preacher took nightly killed herself, and then after the funeral, i saw the boys crouched outside the church, and watched them follow him home, their bodies tracking in and out of the pitch, breaths leading the way. at the preacher's house, they kept quiet. the smaller one stood, face half-lit by the lamppost outside the house, light and wide, his body bending into the shadow. the bigger one didn't look at me, just huddled where he was, rubbing his hands over each other in the pool of light.

i'll get to the point. last i saw, they were walking towards the orchard, following the preacher.

the mayor has the sheriff on the case and there's nothing to chase. so, maybe this will give him something. if he puts things together then good. if not, well, i did my part. but those boys are gone and the last time anyone saw them was that night. it's obvious what happened. people think they went out to the ghost woods. they were talking about it all week. buying drinks and talking. "we're gonna walk through the ghost woods," they kept saying.

ENTER STAGE RIGHT – THE BROTHER'S ROOM

the preacher's brother never wakes
to see the preacher's body at his bedside,

never sees a message left on the backs
and bottoms of things,

only smells the orange and charcoal sifting
around his room in mornings.

this unknots him. and so he goes
to his bible and always reads the first
verse his eyes fall on.

he doesn't see his brother's
message on the back.

when he writes his sermon,
he thinks about his brother, about the way the spirit's

sensation never breached his body, how
he preached hoping to someday

feel that pulsating burn in his limbs.
but he feels something different

when he reads a good verse—
his eyes water and his voice deepens.

EXIT STAGE RIGHT

OFFSTAGE – THE QUIET BOY ATTEMPS TO AVOID KASEY

no. 521
kasey

sidelined by guilt, he stays away from the bar light and jukebox twang, stalks the halls of the hotel, smoking cigarettes, 'cause he's afraid to see kasey again.

she comes around corners, up staircases, down elevator shafts like smoke from a barrel,

claiming all she wants to do is talk.

he's managed to pull himself from sleep before the conversation propels itself forward. but last thursday, she came into the bar and sat next to him, said,

"all i want to do is speak to you…"

so, he's here, stalking, trying to remember if he knows her face from anywhere. but he can't place her.

of the two boys, he's the one who still feels.

he has memorized the feel of the pistol fisted and fired. wakes up sometimes, his hands curled around the phantom of its handle.

this tugs at the inside of his ribcage,

*

the other one sleeps, eats, and talks

about how good it feels to know "the fucker's dead." two days later, he'll slide the paper across the diner table and say, "so, we kind of made the front page."

the law found the murder weapon.

all the found bodies clear things up, piece by piece, shortening the
list, and derailing what started it. "doesn't matter anyway," he says,
chewing on a piece of toast, "body's where no one can dig it up."

      and rain curses the ground. its notes
      sound like:

THE QUIET BOY'S DREAM SEQUENCE

when i slip and tumble into sleep, finally, at the week's end, kasey's
      there, waiting in the flicking light
of a derelict gymnasium. i smell oranges and charcoal. habit kicks in
      and i turn to run, but she yells after me, says,

        "run and i'll find you anyway. it's what i do."

so, i swallow and turn back and cross the hardwood to where she
      stands, follow her out, through sheets
of rain warm as blood, thin as moth wings fluttering down,
      and into buildings of brick and ivy,
through hallways and sliding doors. she keeps saying,

        "not here, not here,"

till we reach a room, windowless and white. she turns, faces me
      and says,

        "when you wake, i'll be behind the tavern,
        waiting."

      *

i snap awake, my hair wet from rainfall, feet stiff from walking,
      and my brother's
fixing coffee, dressed in his underwear, whistling the melody of
      "ode to joy."

i sit up in bed and watch him move through the room,
      sipping coffee,
still whistling, not a speck of remorse coming from anywhere on his
      body.
his face is straight and solid like a piece of dirty glass, and in
      minutes
he's dressed and gone without a word.

        his indifference to our crimes baffles me.
        guilt hits like an anchor skidding across my chest.

SPOTLIGHT CENTER STAGE – THE CONVERSATION

kasey's where she said she'd be, puffing at a cigarette, picking at her nails. she sees him coming up the alley, regret slithering out from every crease of his face, anger boiling under his bones, building, knows it eats at him, tugs at his ribcage, kicks at his chest like an anchor cut free.

and he tries to act natural, to act as though seeing someone from his dreams in front of him is an everyday thing.

*

inside, they find the booth behind the pool tables, in the back corner where smoke and jukebox-twang drowns out whatever conversations need to happen. she's all blue eyes and smiles. when they sit, she says,

> "you're good at keeping things hidden. i know, you've got things to say, and i know you got questions stacked a mile high, but i'm impressed with how calm you seem."

he can smell her and he remembers his dream. he nods, but doesn't speak.

> "first things first, kid. i'm not here for you, i'm here for your brother, the one skipping around town, drinking and picking up women, living off the money you took. him and me, we need to meet. i got words for him."

> "what am i to do?" he says. "i ain't his keeper?"

> "i need to know things about him. i need to know what will open him up. see, he won't let me into his dreams. i stand at the gates and watch him on trains, in banks, on dirt roads, at the helm of wooden boats, with women and men i don't know. i knock and knock on the gates but he won't even look. he just sticks to what he's doing. i need to get his attention."

> "i don't know what to tell you."

"i need you to tell me how to open his gates."

"how the fuck should i know?"

"what silences him?" she says, leaning forward. "what makes him so mad he can't even speak? that'll open him up good and wide."

and for some reason, maybe the way his neck tightens when he thinks of his brother or because to hear his friend's name sends shivers, he says,

"talk about our sister. that's all you can do. guys like him are like blocks of cement. won't even budge unless you go for the only thing he even breathes for. hell, take everything from him he'll be fine, but our sister. he loves that girl. talk about what happened to her."

"what happened to her?"

"they found her body at the bottom of the canyon," he says, leaning closer, so that he can taste her breath, like oranges and charcoal. "you know, down where they found those two queers. her and the baby inside, dead."

"oh," she says, putting things together. "now…you did what i asked. what can i do for you?"

"you can leave me alone," he says, leaning away from her, his eyes watering from the smell. "i just want to sleep."

she just nods twice and sinks away from him, and he's alone, staring across the booth at nothing, the clatter of pool balls crackling and scattering over what the jukebox spits.

EXIT STAGE LEFT

dear sisters,

things have been bleak and the discoveries aren't really leading to answers. the town's kind of on this middle ground between closure and myth. every suspect the sheriff arrests ends up dead in their cell. not murdered. just dead. I didn't want to share this with you, but it's still happening. this morning a woman. last night a man.

but on the other hand morale has risen among the church-goers. the new preacher has put their minds at ease. i don't hear him shouting like the last preacher, but he looks serious when he's at it. outside the bar, i listen to them pass after service, talking about the sermon as if they were sharing it to someone who missed it. when i went, we'd clam up and go to our rooms to pray.

ENTER STAGE LEFT – HOW PREACHERS DIFFER

the preacher's brother
does not present the city as more than a place
filled with trails—
"god," he says, "is in all things,
even the putrid and dark."

he once lived in the eastern cities, knows what pools
in alleys, knows how filth grows where it's left free,
knows where sin nooses and waits.

"do not fear the city. it is not a beast,
it is not the arm of the devil. sin can find us anywhere—
here or the city or out in the orchard.
our duty is to live as we should,
turning from sin, turning without fear."

*

the preacher had things to say
about the cities. sometimes he'd describe a monster,
shiny and concrete,
tied to the leash of the devil,
creeping closer, sprawling from its core
to choke the green and grain
from the earth, to consume
all the churches and their people.

he called buildings more than one floor
"towers of babel,"
and paved roads "the devil's path."
yeah, he'd jeer and seethe as he spoke of this,
cry if people went, and whimper out,
"careful followers, the city fishes for the loving,
disguises its lust as innocence."

*

the congregation nods when the preacher's brother shares,
and in town they speak of city-visits, but

in the walls of their homes
the city is still a monster,
and the preacher is still right.

EXIT STAGE LEFT

ENTER STAGE RIGHT – WHEN THE SHERIFF'S IN TOWN

the business with the preacher has changed
the way the town looks at loss.
they mourn each body without judgment.
they hold funerals that stretch through town,
jazzy songs bursting from the line of people.

the list's been whittled and the sheriff's
still at it, never at these funerals,
never in town for more than a day.
his deputies too.

though, when he's in town, he's not
found at the edge of the ghost woods
or at the blood spot in the orchard that still hasn't
washed away.

lately, he's been patrolling the quarry's
edge, staring down past that
lip, into black that carries
down. he's concerned about the smell
thickening since he brought the first suspect back.

the town's always had this smell, and he knows it,
but never this potent.

when he sees people, he says, "do you smell that?"

and in the cell down the hall from his office,
bodies keep graying.

he can't place its source, but the town
keeps blaming the ghost woods.

he knows it's something else. something keeps
bringing him to the quarry—it tugs at his ribcage.

no answers surface, just new bodies to bury.

EXIT STAGE RIGHT

OFFSTAGE – KASEY ENTERS THE GUILTY BOY'S DREAM

no. 522
kasey

my bodies would rise to watch. i would get over to the next
town and enter his room every night. but his sleep schedule kept
changing. i would find myself waiting for him when the sun rose.
and till his brother gave me his key, i would just stare at him.

or sometimes, i would follow him
around the town.

but today, i enter his room and whisper about his sister into his ear.
it tears at him and jars his entrance, stirs his sleep. the border, once
fogged and blackened out, starts clearing, more doors unlocking.

there's something different with
his dreams.

when he enters the dream he will smell the orange and charcoal, he
will hear the piano across the way from a white room, in the attic
of the town church, as the preacher delivers, like he always does,
sermons.

*

the guilty one enters through a doorway and i start playing.

today, it sounds something like this:

THE GUILTY ONE'S DREAM SEQUENCE – THE CHURCH

i've only been in the church once, back when my mother found me
        out at the quarry throwing rocks at wounded birds,
but it wasn't the kind of church from the pictures, it was colder
        and louder.

so she pulled me out quick and let her hands do the work she
        thought god might, and i'm here again
and the pews ring out like someone started pounding at random
        keys on a piano with fists,

and the floor's on fire, and the preacher's at the pulpit, only he's
        gray and dressed in suede the color of oceans.
he's screaming, "stay where you are. here: god has blessed,"
        then takes a breath like he's drinking water,
and goes, "he has run his fingers through our grain,
        through our pine and fir needles, and sifted
our soil through his palms! look at our crops!" he trembles

                and the pews sprout corn, tomatoes, and
                lemon trees.

"out there, you will not prosper, the city is an animal ready to eat!"
        behind the altar, the pulpit, the cross,
a stairway curls and curls, tightening like a fist, till my head

starts rubbing against the ceiling. i can hear a scale echoing up
        from the pews, octave to octave
and back down. at the top of the stairs, light filters through a
        pinhole, and i want

to see what's through it, so i kick and it ruptures open, and light
        crashes on me, only it's cold and licks at me
like a wave. i have to wipe it from my eyes with my sleeve,
        and through it, a woman sits on a piano
bench, in a room bright as a wedding gown, bare as fresh concrete.
        the scale stops when she lifts her hands
from the keys, and the echo fades. she slams her palms on the low
        end and the sound changes me.
i cower and the piano mutes. from across the room she tells me her

name, kasey. i try to speak, can't,
and she says she's here to show me what guilt is, to teach me
how to be a real man,
to give me what i deserve, and the piano swells

and floats and starts playing a progression,
tied to a cadence i think i've heard before.

dear sisters,

the fog has lifted today, but from my window i can see the ghost woods' shape in the gray mass. there are figures moving around, maybe wolves, maybe people, maybe the dead coming back to haunt us, waiting for the fog to reach the meat of town.

it's sunday and i can't hear the preacher's brother. he's too quiet, and the town's only gotten louder. in an hour, they'll leave the church, screaming about what was said.

yesterday, the church-folk found a body. the sheriff seemed distant, seemed hazy, as though he was somewhere else, when he crouched in front of her. this was the girl who claimed to have survived the ghost woods. she told people it wasn't that scary, that it was peaceful, and that she would've walked right through it, but there was a big concrete wall at the back with ropes dangling down from the darkness of higher branches. i never heard that story from her lips, but bar-talk did the job.

her name never made the list. i saw her yesterday, walking through town.

SPOTLIGHT UPSTAGE RIGHT – THE MURDER WEAPON

the murder weapon gets discovered barrel up and half-rusted
in the swamp water
at the north end of the river.

this is where the drug smugglers from the south of mexico were
busted and carried off last november. they spoke in spanish, rattling
off sentences, kicking at the officers till they were shoved into their
cell.

a junkie on her last leg
went to sink the needle's teeth into the black
sore hidden under shirt sleeves, down
in the nook of her arm.
yeah, she found it before she could push off—
did it anyway.

      the sheriff had questions for her
      but she had no answers,
      just shrugs and hand motions.

      he finds the trail anyway, and waits
      with his deputies in the motel, three rooms down,
      loading bullets into their chambers.

this is how the boys' plans get shot to hell—

their visions of concrete stretching out as highways, into the arms
of the western states, and golden gates parting, opening up to
freedom and fame—yanked back from their grips at four a.m.,
when the motel door flies open, off its hinges. bodies in black pour
in, filling the room, waving their barrels.

one boy lies still and quiet, his body gray,
arms folded over his chest, just like the others.
kasey had come.

the other simply sits up in bed, arms out, ready for the shackles.

CURTAIN FALLS

dear sisters,

i've been here a year. a year's long enough.

it may be a good while before i write again. after i send this, i'll find the first train, climb into an empty boxcar and take it north. in the city, i'll find myself a new job. i don't care what it is.

i'm leaving 'cause i can't take the unfolding of people and their families every time a body is found. last i heard, the list has been cut in half. there's a pressure in town. people look at each other differently, as though all of these murders means that the town isn't safe anymore. every suspect ends up dead. i heard that once they go to sleep in the cell, they won't wake. i didn't believe it, but for the last couple days i've been watching the sheriff's office. i've watched the deputies carry out three bodies in the last four days.

and the smell.

it clears the bars on thursday nights, clears the street on saturdays so no one can smell what the shops are cooking. you'd practically have to shove your nose in a loaf of bread to smell it. it's gotten so bad that the followers make themselves nose plugs to wear during service.

the smell is the worst inside, thick as syrup and chalk in there, as if there are piles of orange peels and lumps of charcoal filling the pews.

the worst part? people keep talking about the ghost woods.

EPILOGUE – THE CURTAIN RISES AND SPOTLIGHT FOLLOWS THE ACTION

there's a funeral procession coursing through the meat of town.

ENTER STAGE RIGHT – FUNERAL SOUNDS

the frenzy settles, but the sheriff and his deputies
are still at it,
the list filling with x after x.

the preacher gets his funeral.

there is no organ,
no piano, just followers
singing hymns between words, singing
hymns as they carry
the casket from the church to the graveyard.

the non-believers watch them from windows
and porches
and stoops, impressed by the spectacle.

by sundown, the hymns have settled into silence
and all that stands
left is the night's hum—crickets and canyon
echo, and the wolves tracking their prey.

the town has grown
tired of funerals,
both believers and non-believers.

and people say,
"the ghost woods wait."

LIGHTS DOWN

CURTAIN FALLS

THIS
IS THE WAY
TO RULE

LEADER – Gray-haired. In his early 70s. Constantly tired, but nothing scares or surprises him.

SURVIVORS – We do not know who survives this.

AIDES & ADVISORS – They speak for the gods.

GENERAL – He leads nations to war.

DJ – We hear them on the airwaves. They tell stories. They preach.

SOLDIERS – They burn & kill & die.

CHILDREN – They do not understand the pain.

GHOSTS – They have not killed the one(s) responsible.

VOICE – Possibly the voice of god(s) or a psychotic break. Imaginary?

PREACHER – Just a preacher.

it's not fiction speaking to me from quiet places. what noiselessness unfolds when the deed's done. & it is darker. it lends ideas about what it means to be good. / in the cities, silence only comes for tragedy. we would don hoods to shade our faces, stir up dust, haunt the alley mouths. / this responsibility unleashed on us we bumped at it, till we could no longer breathe, till our appendages hurt. / in my vision before the visit the world buckled in & they came from above us, two floors maybe, & they were spiraling & burrowing till they breached the doorway & stopped in the hallway to settle before the change. / it's dark in there where reality lands—slabs of night had been stripped & laid inside as though they were mortared with tar & pine. sound gets caught between the edges. where it's said, dialogue from decades back bangs up against what i let slip. / i feel as though it's coming—as though i must pay for my decisions. but what fault am i at for leveraging what i need to keep the towers happy. / this is about legacy, my legacy, & i must make decisions based on sustaining the diamond gleam my name produces.

SCENE I

CURTAIN RISES revealing a SPOTLIGHT on an EMPTY ROOM. Outside the light, there is darkness covering an entire nation. It is night. There are mountains & plains & roads & rivers & lakes & homes & deserts & suburbs & cities & malls & people. There are many peoples.

LEADER sits at his desk under the light. He stares out the window. The moon glows in the window. He is quiet.

The sound of life MURMURS from the other side of the walls—phones, conversation, footsteps, laughter, copy machines.

Moments pass.

Suddenly the roof bursts open & a MASSIVE SHAFT OF LIGHT pummels into the room. Covering everything like oil. The room becomes crooked. It loosens.

LEADER rises from his desk & stumbles through the room, fighting for balance. The room unlevels, lifts up, throws him to the floor, then shoves him up against the wall & back to the ground.

Time slacks, begins sifting. The space swells & stretches where it can.

> VOICE *(from the shaft of light)* young men, praise the suffering!

A gaggle of YOUNG MEN enter the room. They are dressed as OFFICE AIDES, but glow & there are clearly wings under their blazers.

> YOUNG MEN *(sung)* ba-ba-baaaaaaaaaaaaaaaaaaaaaaaaaaaaaa aaaaaaaaaaaaaaaaaaaaaaaaaaaaaaaaaaaaaaaaahhhhhhhhhhhhhh hhhhhhhhhhhhhhhhhhhhhhhhhhhhhhhhhhhhhhhhhhhhhhhhhh

> LEADER *(shouting over the YOUNG MEN)* conversations get lost in the creases & corners. i would gather them later, when they finally quiet—

VOICE *(from the shaft of light)* young women, praise the suffering!

A gaggle of YOUNG WOMEN enter the room. They are dressed as OFFICE AIDES, but glow & there are clearly wings under their blazers.

YOUNG WOMEN *(harmonizing with the YOUNG MEN)* ba-ba-baaaaaaaaaaaaaaaaaaaaaaaaaaaaaaaaaaaaaaaaaaaaaaaaaaaaa aaaaaaaaaaaaaaaaaaaaaaaaaaaaaaaaaaaahhhhhhhhhhhhhhhhhh hhhhhhhhhhhhhhhhhhhhhhhhhhhhhhhhhhhhhhhhhhhhhhhhhh

The room parts down the middle, dividing the YOUNG MEN from the YOUNG WOMEN, & the room begins to shake violently. The YOUNG MEN & WOMEN throw themselves across the divide & begin stripping themselves / each other till they are sharing each others' bodies.

The room spins quickly.
We can only see the actions through a window.
The room aches.

Outside, WIND slams against the walls.

Inside, the YOUNG MEN & WOMEN keep at it.

LEADER is frozen in time. Standing there.

The WIND throws bottles at the wall.
Bottles' mouths kissing the window frames.

VOICE *(from the shaft of light)* old men, curse the suffering!

A clot of OLD MEN enter the room. They are dressed as ADVISORS, but glow & there are clearly wings under their blazers.

OLD MEN *(octave higher than the YOUNG MEN & WOMEN)* ba-ba-baaaaaaaaaaaaaaaaaaaaaaaaaaaaaaaaaaaaaaaaaa aaaaaaaaaaaaaaaaaaahhhhhhhhhhhhhhhhhhhhhhhhhhhhhhh

LEADER *(yelling over the OLD MEN)* i'm not interested in the silence before notes, but the tempo slowly ratcheting

197

tighter—

VOICE *(from the shaft of light)* old women, curse the suffering!

A clot of OLDER WOMEN enter the room. They are dressed in business suits, but glow & clearly have wings under their blazers.

OLDER WOMEN *(harmonizing with OLD MEN)* ba-ba-baaaaaaaaaaaaaaaaaaaaaaaaaaaaaaaaaaaaaaaaaaaaaaaaaaa aaaaaaaaaaaaaaaaaaaaaaaaaaaahhhhhhhhhhhhhhhhhhhhh hhhhhhhhhhhhhhhhhhhhhhhhhhhhhhhhhhhhhhhhhhhhhhhh

The OLD MEN & OLDER WOMEN do as the YOUNG MEN & WOMEN do.

LEADER i do not understand these metaphors. please speak clearly.

The room coughs, throwing the MEN & WOMEN across the room out the window, into the backyard of decades' leftovers.

The sofa shreds & the fabric follows the MEN & WOMEN, covering their naked bodies if only momentarily.

The walls strip & follow. They sing, a half-step up.

OLDER WOMEN ba-ba-baaaaaaaaaaaaaaaaaaaaaahhhhhhh hhhhhhhhhhhhhhhhhhhhhhhhhhhhhhhhhhhhhhhhhhhhhhhh

OLD MEN ba-ba-baaaaaaaaaaaaaaaaaaaaaaaaaaaaaahhhhhhh hhhhhhhhhhhhhhhhhhhhhhhhhhhhhhhhhhhhhhhhhhhhhhhh

YOUNG MEN ba-ba-baaaaaaaaaaaaaaaaaaaaaaaaahhhhhhh hhhhhhhhhhhhhhhhhhhhhhhhhhhhhhhhhhhhhhhhhhhhhhhh

YOUNG WOMEN ba-ba-baaaaaaaaaaaaaaaaaaaaaahhhhhh hhhhhhhhhhhhhhhhhhhhhhhhhhhhhhhhhhhhhhhhhhhhhhhh

These four choruses continue & LEADER attempts to speak over them.

LEADER (*pretending he can't understand, screaming over them*) i am not listening because i cannot hear you & i cannot understand you. i am not listening because i cannot hear you & i cannot understand you. i am not listening because i cannot hear you & i cannot understand you. i am not listening because i cannot hear you & i cannot understand you. i am not listening because i cannot hear you & i cannot understand you. i am not listening because i cannot hear you & i cannot understand you. i am not listening because i cannot hear you & i cannot understand you. i am not listening because i cannot hear you & i cannot understand you. i am not listening because i cannot hear you & i cannot understand you. i am not listening because i cannot hear you & i cannot understand you. i am not listening because i cannot hear you & i cannot understand you. i am not listening because i cannot hear you & i cannot understand you. i am not listening because i cannot hear you & i cannot understand you. i am not listening because i cannot hear you & i cannot understand you. i am not listening because i cannot hear you & i cannot understand you. i am not listening because i cannot hear you & i cannot understand you. i am not listening because i cannot hear you & i cannot understand you. i am not listening because i cannot hear you & i cannot understand you.

STAGE LIGHTS DOWN.

We still hear them—the four choruses & LEADER, then—

The sound of RUMBLING fills the theater. It is so loud the speakers DISTORT.

SILENCE.

A DOG BARKS.

A BIRD CHIRPS.

A COUGH.

dear survivors,

in the bruised light of dawn, when birds begin those steady single notes, piano-like, we rise from the rubble. the city is all piles & spires of smoke, as though someone had plunged their hand into the center & yanked. we mourn alone & gather where highways used to merge.

SCENE II

A SOFT DIM LIGHT slowly lights the back corner of the stage. The light is bright enough to show a desk, but dark enough so that the rest of the stage is covered in such a dimness it's like the light is a film covering everything.

DJ enters from upstage & walks through the dim light to the desk. They flip on the desk lamp & REVEAL a small radio booth with a large microphone, archaic equipment, & cords wrapped & knotted & tangled. We are in a massive empty room. DJ walks to a full bookcase on the back wall & pulls off a book, reads, then puts it back.

DJ goes to the desk. Sigh. They press some buttons, expertly, but patiently. A red light BUZZES on above their head. They lean forward, speaking into the microphone.

DJ *(speaking quietly, but forcefully, urgently in a way)* the capital. this is the source. this is where the WRECKAGE started. the rot was constructed. the parade was fierce, clicking out its own calls. no one's face went cold & we could reach the confused. *(picking up emotional momentum till they are all but yelling at the end, spit flying from their mouth when they get to the last line. but the thing is, it's not yelling. they are still quiet. it's as though they need people to hear this, but are afraid to match the content with the volume. that said, we can feel the intended yells in their delivery. we know that this is important. we know that they mean every word.)* bound by our desires to remain inferior, we gave into the pull, gave into the passing of time, press-ganged between our safety & a possible stronghold, disintegration comes from our hands, through the pores. the creases, slow as laws passing, this left us to our half-empty bivouac, between tumbled bricks & mortar & shells. the venom has loosed itself into the country & the wires connecting us have been cut. after all, we put him there.

DJ clears their throat. Looks around. Startled by something we cannot hear, they rise & hurry away from the desk & INTO THE DARK.

We wait. They return, relaxed. Sit. Begin again.

DJ the WRECKAGE left us amputated. *(big sigh)* someone says they heard there were more cities, south & west of here, getting the treatment. then we hear soldiers piling through the mouth of our city, but there are no orders or gunshots. they march from one end to the other. they do not look at us. but i can feel their hate slipping around on the outside of our homes. they're up to something.

STAGE LIGHTS DIM. Only the red light BUZZES. Then it goes off.

In the darkness, FOOTSTEPS leave the stage.

dear survivors,

some of our children are in other cities. there is only one
phone booth still standing, out at the rail station, but there
it's only clicks & static.

dear survivors,

when the rain came, dragging black tendrils from the clouds, we climbed up to the caves above the city & watched. in the morning fog came, covered the place where the city used to lay, covered the harbor over the next bluff, but now the fog has opened, first as a slit through the center, & there are ships in the harbor, tilted into the water or capsized or knocking against the shoreline. there are no sailors, just specks of white waves. our voices echo off the cliff walls & below us in our city there are soldiers, abandoned by the fog-cover. they set what's left of our avenues & homes on fire. they set fire & go, south. an hour later, the ships are burning, the harbor is burning. we retreat south, into the woods.

dear survivors,

we rest in an untouched field miles from the city. around us, the sound of WRECKAGE finds other towns, just west. by dusk, the air smells of diesel & aluminum, & another fire throbs through the trees sweeping the dark away. the muscles of the town flay, its brick & concrete scattered under the flames, its bodies burning, its water towers uncorked, spilling into the heat. when we arrive survivors watch the fires feed. they do not like our presence, ask us to leave. we push south, where a hill shakes, its lights swaying, dropping, till extinguished.

SCENE III

SPOTLIGHT UPSTAGE on an untouched field, surrounded by trees green & thick from spring.

A group of survivors rests in the tall grass.

There is a RUMBLING /

the sound of WRECKAGE

moving from OFFSTAGE LEFT

to RIGHT then quieting.

After a few moments a spire of smoke rises.

The SURVIVORS do not speak.

They watch the spire turn into a cloud.

They rise & move—

back into the trees.

dear survivors,

only the edges of this valley caught the fury of the WRECKAGE. the wet, clouded sky-line kept the fires from the center. & here, this place is intact & there are doors & raccoons walking sidewalks. we climb through an open grocery store window & stock up on food, eat till we're full. we do not want to leave, but know this will still be waiting if we have to come back.

dear survivors,

we reach the hill in the darkest parts of morning, but the
city cratered & we only see the afterwards. the soldiers find
the crater, & though there is nothing left to burn, they do
it anyway. we huddle in the woods, watching them light
& retreat. to the east, where skyscrapers itch the skyline,
WRECKAGE. the soldiers move towards the sound. we follow.
at the city's edge, there are no soldiers, but a fire so big it has
hips & shoulders, spiraling out & out. we attempt to put it
out, but it keeps digging in & taking swings. by morning,
there is only a stretch of ashes & coal, a black plain. at night,
there are fires dotted in the dark.

SCENE IV

SPOTLIGHT STAGE LEFT

SURVIVORS stand inside a department store. They are surrounded by leftover XL coats. Another group of SURVIVORS, smaller, with more children, enter from the darkness of the stage. They are holding coats with faux-fur & thick lining. They are unreasonably clean—

SURVIVOR please take these. you may need them.

SURVIVOR please come with us.

SURVIVOR we are safe & comfortable here. the last earthquake put a hole in the grocery store next door. we have food for years.

SURVIVOR the ones who left will come back & the soldiers will come back too.

SURVIVOR the soldiers passed. they could not set anything on fire. they tried for an entire day & gave up. the flame just wouldn't catch.

SURVIVOR there is no one left. everyone but us perished in the earthquakes.

SURVIVOR enters with a tray of food. Hands food to the SURVIVOR.

SURVIVOR eat, then be on your way.

SURVIVOR we were hoping to stay the night. we don't quite know our way in the dark.

SURVIVOR we're sorry, but you cannot stay. just follow the fires.

SURVIVOR but that's where the soldiers are.

SURVIVOR you're not chasing the soldiers?

SURVIVOR no.

SURVIVOR you can't stay here.

DARKNESS.

In the distance, the orange glow of fires burn.

dear survivors,

in really small towns, there are brown signs with arrows. CEMETERY they say, as if passers-by have to know others had lived & died here. though, now, we can see that the towns have become their own cemeteries.

dear survivors,

there are so many bodies & the stench is heavy. men in the basement of the mill say that sleep hit the whole room & they tried to wake their friends, but couldn't, & the shaking came. that's what they call it, *the shaking*.

dear survivors,

during the night, we passed through a tunnel right before the summit. there was no other way through & the WRECKAGE already tore through everything but the tunnel & hadn't been heard in hours. our lanterns cleared a path through the up-ahead. there were thousands of empty spray cans covering the ground inside. different colors, their caps separate & scattered, cracked & chipped. our feet clinked & cracked through the mess. on the walls there were drawings covering every inch from the ground to the other side. pictures of the ghosts of this nation. not real ghosts. ghosts of novels & films & poems. we saw henry & sal & nick. white ghosts. all doing their thing. each face exaggerated in size, shape, & color. their eyes were lighthouses. there was one man, his gray beard & green eyes attracted the lantern-light. at the end of the tunnel, we turned around when we heard rain. we made a fire in the center, & as we cooked & ate, we stared at the paintings. someone said, "you think when this is all over, people will paint over this?" no one wanted to answer. we let our fire crackle. no soldiers came.

SCENE A

Standing in a grove of fruit trees—SURVIVORS wander around in the shade & pluck fruit from the tress. The sun beats the uncovered hills out ahead. This feels like the first time they have a moment of pleasantry. It's as if the world is unchanged. Then in the distance—WRECKAGE.

SURVIVOR sounds like a demolition crew.

SURVIVOR sounds like towers falling.

SURVIVOR sounds like god weeding a city of its metal & concrete.

SURVIVOR sounds like bombs shaking.

SURVIVOR sounds like nothing we've heard.

SURVIVOR sounds like—

SURVIVOR sounds—

SURVIVOR sound—

dear survivors,

the WRECKAGE here is so incredible, so massive that when the city toppled it became a landslide & carried limbs of each avenue into the ocean. from the beach it looks as though a city grew from the sea, half-drunk & ambitious to spread, cobbling structures as fast as possible, anchored to the hillside as secondhand ruins. there are no survivors & the soldiers are uncovering what they can, looking for survivors. we see bodies floating next to what slid into the ocean. the soldiers do not see us. they do not find survivors. they start fires.

dear survivors,

as we round the veer, we catch the back-end of a garrison. they've gathered & camped. we panic & double back into the woods. for hours we wait for them to come for us. at twilight, we hear laughter & fire-talk. we approach, all quiet, to watch them. maybe out of curiosity, maybe out of stupidity, maybe out of the need to see other human beings—we haven't seen another breathing human for weeks now—but they aren't laughing. the fire is whimpering, barely. their faces are stuck in stares. they're dead. we hear movement in the tree line & scatter forward towards the next town.

SCENE V

SURVIVORS stand at the MOUTH of a PARKING GARAGE. The night is noir-ish, cutting across their bodies. In the shadows, ANOTHER GROUP OF SURVIVORS stand. We can see their faces plucked from the dark.

SURVIVORS we huddled in my basement when we heard it come. out the windows there were people scattering for cover, so we took to the basement. we heard our things slamming around. decades ago my grandfather heard the word nuclear & built this basement barely six feet deep, but as wide as the foundation. after a radio broadcast, he hobbled to the back laundry room, tore up the carpet, & started digging, but the cold war never reached its potential & nothing detonated. what he built to protect from the bomb & fallout, we reserved for my children's old clothes & toys, my wife's paintings & wardrobes & jewelry, my forgotten hobbies—casio keyboards, guitars, & nintendos— and it became the space to wait out the shaking. but when the soldiers came they came for my place. i fled before the sparks caught, made my way through the wall of smoke that became this town. & here we are. this is where we'll stay. the soldiers have left. they won't be back.

dear survivors,

we're on a hill on the crest between two cities—it's like they're breeding. they look the same, but they're not. these soldiers have been called to where they're needed. there are garrisons & gatherings everywhere. different people.

dear survivors,

people used to sit on this bench & watch the sunset. everything is just filed down. this bench looks polished. it shines in the gray-light. the ocean clicks rocks together. sounds like the echo of a piano restrung. we sit & try to imagine what the sunset used to look like from here. a fire swells behind us. the soldiers are near. we find cover in the far bushes on the other side of the stream. when they're gone we uncover & put it out.

dear survivors,

someone says, "everything's still standing." we came in the
backside of town, where the buildings & streets love to
collect rust & dirt & broken things. & we start peering
down alleys. there are no stop lights ripped sideways, no
pipes bursting, no creviced roads. the rust & wear is natural.

then the WRECKAGE comes.

we should've known, but people say this side of town has
been known to play tricks on travelers. an avalanche of steel
& glass & concrete begins to cascade ahead of us, where the
city grows. then the gas hisses & the street crevices & the
main breaks. a violating roar & the force creating ruins. we
turn to escape, but there is a line of soldiers a few blocks
away, toeing the edge of town. they watch us.

then they set a fire. it blazes towards us. we crawl into a
bus that has tipped on its side. the street keeps splitting &
it pulls things into its mouth. the bus starts sliding, but its
guts catch us, holding us above the surface. we stare down
into the mouth of gas & trinkets of the WRECKAGE getting
swallowed. the fire comes faster now, catching the gas &
swinging where it can. we're jammed in the bus, the doors
caught. we start kicking at the glass till it breaks or pulps.
when the fire's upon us, we crawl through the hole where
glass used to be. we retreat forward, into the still-simmering
WRECKAGE. the fire chasing. there's no way to put it out. all
we can do is run.

SCENE B

A small fire CENTER STAGE.

A gathering of SOLDIERS huddled around it, eating beans out of cans & jerky out of bags. They're covered in ash & rubble-dust. We can see 10-15, & others sleep at the fringes of the fire's light. The awake ones speak:

SOLDIER still don't know what we're doing.

SOLDIER orders—

SOLDIER the cities are wrecked.

SOLDIER the blood.

SOLDIER we've seen blood before.

SOLDIER we didn't make the blood this time.

SOLDIER we do what we're ordered.

SOLDIER what do these fires hide?

SOLDIER your questions…please…

SOLDIER questions are stacking up.

dear survivors,

we didn't see the soldiers when we came down the trail, too
in love with the way it smelled of pine & lake-water.

the lake spread out in front of us, the moon's reflection
rippled at the far end. we made camp, but smelled sulfur. &
up at the mouth of the trail, a small red dot paced through
the dark. it lowered & sat. the lake's surface looked red &
orange when the fire rose. it covered the moon. the fire
trembled down the hill.

soldiers set it & came for us. we moved back, into the
shallows, holding our things above our heads. we were
ankle-deep & the fire purged in front of us till it met where
the sand meets the dirt & moss. it burned hours & all that
was left was the blackened wood spikes of what used to be a
forest & lumps of charcoal.

above, where the fire started, there were no dead soldiers,
but a recent camp had gone vacant, food wrappers & cans
left as evidence.

we set forth, towards the next town.

dear survivors,

we come upon a party of women cutting through the gut of a forest. when they see us approaching, they scatter. we keep shouting, "we mean no harm, we mean no harm!" but just as quickly as we came upon them, they've vanished. we can hear breaths & twigs snapping, but cannot see them. our shouts keep echoing, further & further into the trees.

dear survivors,

this was a diner where all the hipsters used to smoke their cigarettes & drink their coffee & think about the bands they had discovered. now it's a shelter, the only dry place in town with a roof & fire hydrants outside. people cram themselves behind the glass & steel & watch the rain kill the fires attempting to take what's left. someone says, "we didn't need the hydrants after all." someone else laughs.

dear survivors,

for some reason, in every town, the schools are the first to become piles & the churches are the first to burn. we don't notice till today, when we see what the soldiers' sequel was. this one-road town had only schools, a church, & a gas station-diner. the diner stands. the church is burnt & the schools are piles. we don't know what they are when we first see them, but their signs at the road are still standing. someone says, "always the schools."

SCENE VI

DJ is still on air, speaking into the microphone, the red light BUZZING.

> DJ some say this started the WRECKAGE, but we know it
> came south after the soldiers started the fires. some say it
> came from the palm of a man, who got the shaking from
> god's finger. we can't know, but i'm sure the intention wasn't
> good, i'm sure the intention wasn't grand. & when it started,
> no inventor could cork what was coming, & before anything
> could be done, the spreading began.

DJ leans away. Takes a sip of water, then leans back to the microphone.

> DJ listen: there will be v o i c e s rising & falling &
> b e n d i n g through a l l e y s. kids' faces go cold
> when the gates open. some call them story thieves. really
> they're people who lie about where they came from. *(long
> pause)* listen: this isn't a math equation, this comes from the
> gut. it's something black that rises when it's summoned. i've
> got my own story, but it won't sell.

dear survivors,

don't know what this was about, but the pond is full of bodies. they're plump & waterlogged. either someone dumped them days ago or they all came down to the river to drown themselves. i remember a movie i saw years & years ago, where a line of people in white marched serenely through the obese heat of summer to be baptized. they sang & sang & sang, a chorus of a capella. & one by one they were dunked & cleansed. but i don't imagine that's what happened to them. not after what we've seen. i keep picturing that scene though. then i imagine the preacher dunking these men & women, & not letting them up. they kick & struggle, but he won't let them up. then they cease & he lets them float away. i wonder if god feels like this. he's just letting us float away. there isn't a town for miles, nor sign of the WRECKAGE. but here are hundreds of dead. someone finds an old church bus on the other side of the pond. it's empty, but someone left a note: GO FORTH, it says.

dear survivors,

we slide around the aorta for months, plucking through the
brick & concrete of toppled walls & dissolving foundations.
what brought the air to throttling cities?

dear survivors,

the wind starts swinging for anything. screen doors are creaking & snapping at the frame. swing sets wheeze. branches drag against each other. we're all ushering memories forward & telling stories, but they're weaved together with the scent the fire brings. some of us are weeping, some of us are singing. when there's nothing else to do, we talk. that's what we do when we're not moving, putting out fires, running. no one wants to investigate that. someone mentions the capitol, someone mentions rebuilding. we are looking for other survivors. we've been at it for—what? a month, maybe two. who knows, calendars are useless—the sky is dark gray. the next morning we pull out our compasses & head for the capitol. our hope elates us. we course through the trail of WRECKAGE, city after city, landscape after landscape.

SCENE [ ]

The ghost-dance. We cannot see them dance. They dance outside of time.

Two GHOSTS enter our time—they move across the stage as though untethered by gravity, but curious with its mechanics. They stay low, but move with passions.

We cannot hear what they hear, but they move.

Then they dance back out of time. We wait. They dance, but we cannot see them.

They enter our time again for a moment just to play, to pretend to live with gravity—till they disappear outside our time again.

OFFSTAGE, SOLDIERS gather at the edge of a city, perched on a hill. The sun rises behind them. SOLDIERS douse the buildings & roads & cars & WRECKAGE with gasoline, with whatever they have—it reeks worse than gasoline, but it looks of it. SOLDIERS keep at it. Silhouettes up there.

OFFSTAGE (ACROSS THE STAGE), SURVIVORS drag themselves through a thick wood. They are moving towards the city. They will reach the stage & cross it. They will not see the ghost-dance. They will move away towards the city, perched on the hill.

When they arrive the fire will be chewing.

SOLDIERS will have already moved on.

SURVIVORS keep pushing thick branches out of their trail. It's so thick. They are slowing. If there were fewer trees they would reach the city before the fire does too much damage. But the trees are so thick & no fire has touched them. They are old & strong & we can only hope the fire does not find them.

dear survivors,

it's clear we can't help every town. already we've had to double-time to keep up. there are stones rattling & crashing to our lefts & rights every hour, maybe half hour, but we keep on the mains. we go where most people might be. some survivors spread out to help neighboring places. we warn them of the soldiers setting fires. they warn us of the ghost-killings.

dear survivors,

our eyes fight to stay open, but we keep on, our bodies resting at intervals, working through the aching—we all feel it. this is not a vacation, this is what it means to rescue. we've found routine in this destruction. we rotate, each of us trying to catch a few hours, but we keep waking, dreaming about the fires, about the heat crawling & the bodies underneath.

dear survivors,

this morning we woke to the distant clanging of a church bell, & hours later we came upon it, toppled & on its side— we can picture the collapse, the sound grasping for echoes.

someone clangs it with a rock & says, "time for church."

another says, "there might be wine inside."

we drink a bottle between ourselves & carry more along. it feels good to have wine swishing in our bellies. the temperature plummets at twilight & we punch through that dark curtain with burning guts & half-dizzy heads.

SURVIVORS huddle in a cave.

They speak of their old lives. The nostalgia so heavy they sink into the ground. They keep at it. Become so filled with nostalgia that it begins to coat their bodies, it brings them to tears—everything has been so muted, expected, that this moment <u>feels</u>.

They let themselves open, turning into wounds.

They stare out of the cave into the chalky night, post-fire.

STAGE RIGHT a SOLDIER crawls under a patch of SPOTLIGHT. He desperately crawls away from the curtains. Something follows that we cannot see. He crawls out of the light.

There are no other SOLDIERS ONSTAGE or anywhere. He is alone.

Quiet.

Crawling.

His body urging itself forward towards some faux-safety.

dear survivors,

there are two middle-aged women, hair streaked gray, standing in the courtyard of a hotel. they're protecting a clot of toddlers sucking on pacifiers & crawling around a clearing made in the rubble. they're cut, bruised, & smeared with shades of filth, but they're not crying. one of the women says there hasn't been crying since thursday, says it'd do no good bringing their parents back.

SCENE VII

TIME — AFTERNOON

SURVIVORS lie in the middle of a highway that has been reduced to what resembles a gravel road. The asphalt has broken & scattered everywhere. There are felled trees & broken-down cars upturned & upright & on their sides & telephone poles & light poles.

SURVIVORS lie against a car, sliding down—their heads rest against the tires.

SURVIVORS enter & move cautiously towards the SURVIVORS, looking around.

> SURVIVOR *(to the SURVIVORS)* they're gone now. they're gone.

The SURVIVORS move closer. They stop, look around, move again.

> SURVIVOR *(shouting over to the SURVIVORS)* they're long gone.

> SURVIVOR what happened?

> SURVIVOR those soldiers didn't like what we were saying, what we were doing.

> SURVIVOR they're not good at liking things.

> SURVIVOR just, you know, just be here. *(pauses, thinking)* we were all over this shit, just looking for a place to settle & there were eagles sky-locked on the pass, smoke filling the blue. everyone else had let it go. but we couldn't. we let it stew. we saw the soldiers & we started chasing them, not really chasing, but sort of calling out at them, & they didn't like that we were calling them murderers & machines, they didn't like that we told them how many people have died, they didn't like that we said they were evil.

> SURVIVOR we haven't met a good soldier.

SURVIVOR no no no no no. it wasn't like that. a telephone pole plummeted from back there & knocked a wall near us & some metal & glass took a jab or two. *(pausing in pain)* one of the soldiers came over & helped me. the other soldiers were yelling at him to leave us, to hurry up, that we were nothing, but this dude, he just looked at us like we mattered & he apologized & we could tell he meant it. but he had to go. we understood. we understand. you'll have to go too, but just stand here & let us pass, & put our bodies somewhere where there's a good view, where those eagles might fly over.

SURVIVORS agree. They stand there as the SURVIVORS slowly pass away. When they're not breathing, SURVIVORS pick up the bodies & carry them OFFSTAGE, towards where the good hills are.

dear survivors,

we've stopped marveling at the WRECKAGE's backdrop, even when the gray sky cuts up & gets golden & bruised, silhouetting the wounded cities, even when the roads crack & sweat & crumble, laying out jagged hunks of metal & stone. but we marvel at this:

it's as if someone has gathered all the dead soldiers in the area & arranged their bodies side by side along the shoulder, towards the horizon. there's a trail through the center of bodies—hundreds—and as we move, bodies keep appearing on the horizon. when the pitch of night drapes over us, we can feel the limbs brushing our ankles & feet.

dear survivors,

everything shook & rose. the horizon's line bent & swayed.
the mess at our feet ribboned up our bodies. the heaps of
relics of the modern age split & leveled out, forming a plain
of WRECKAGE. we were gone before the soldiers set fires, but
in the unbroken black we could smell them trailing behind
us.

dear survivors,

the sun dove hours ago. the night is cloaked. the night is exhaustive. derelicts of light burn pinholes in the distant ebony, but they remain evasive, unlighting as we approach, mirage-like. still reeling from 14 fires we shellacked over the week, our spirits are potent. though this is the case, we do not sing or converse, we throttle forward into the black.

SCENE SOMETHING OR OTHER

An old, gutted diner space, halfway through a remodel—the project abandoned during the disaster—plastic wrapped around everything, hanging from the doors & windows. Obviously, it is a mess, but the mess is not from the WRECKAGE.

SOLDIER we need to get to work.

SOLDIER we need to rest.

SOLDIER we used to come here & just fuck around & smoke & eat fries & talk about our futures.

SOLDIER we need to get back to work.

SOLDIER do you have the fuel?

SOLDIER …

SOLDIER we need to get up & go. there's work.

SOLDIER …

dear survivors,

this silence comes after fruitless attempts to scale the ridge & smother a fire. the WRECKAGE shook us from our footholds & the fires chewed.

dear survivors,

a year ago, this stretch of commerce sprawled from its core—corporate chains & tourists clogging up the lanes— but today it's empty. clumps of concrete & brick throated into a new chasm lining the roadside.

dear survivors,

the blistered light of early fall. our path from city to city knots & loosens depending on the wind's direction & the cold's touch. the streets in the outskirts become unnamed & untethered, botched by the fire's work or the WRECKAGE making rounds, & ahead a city goes ablaze & lets go the smoke. the next day, we taste it with our meals. we move fast, but we cannot douse the flames—this goes unsaid, but must be said: this is when we become somber, when we cannot douse them.

SCENE VIII

The red light does not BUZZ. DJ stands at the bookcase flipping through the journals. Skims. Closes the book. Puts it back. Picks up another one. Repeat. They do this six times.

On the sixth one, a small cassette tape falls out. They bend & pick it up. They examine it.

They walk over to their equipment & put the cassette in a stereo. The stereo plays. DJ listens, sort of walks around.

> RECORDING i've made a name for myself, pulling our mast through the marbled fog—the lighthouse toppled over a year back, when children came from the outskirts, their only possessions hanging from their necks. they came to frame its fall. afterwards, back in their homes, they put pictures in cut-out squares of cardboard & hung them along hallways. each home offers one snap in the series. to get the scene, you'd have to walk through the town, house to house, to see it. most just look at the last one, when the thing had settled. i heard some hung from the deck, their feet dangling over the rocks & water. at night, the bridge blinks at us from its stretch through the black horizon, lights coursing across it. below, ships caught in the current grope through the water till they slam into the pilings or cliffsides. sometimes, sailors will rise from the waves. we've found their treasures in the sand, waterlogged books & hats, trinkets from the other places, where cities still stand.

The tape goes silent. Tape fuzz. That analog BUZZ.

DJ walks over. REWINDS. Flips a switch.

The red light BUZZES.

They hit play on the stereo. They stand up, listening again as it plays.

> RECORDING i've made a name for myself, pulling our

mast through the marbled fog—the lighthouse toppled over a year back, when children came from the outskirts, their only possessions hanging from their necks. they came to frame its fall. afterwards, back in their homes, they put pictures in cut-out squares of cardboard & hung them along hallways. each home offers one snap in the series. to get the scene, you'd have to walk through the town, house to house, to see it. most just look at the last one, when the thing had settled. i heard some hung from the deck, their feet dangling over the rocks & water. at night, the bridge blinks at us from its stretch through the black horizon, lights coursing across it. below, ships caught in the current grope through the water till they slam into the pilings or cliffsides. sometimes, sailors will rise from the waves. we've found their treasures in the sand, waterlogged books & hats, trinkets from the other places, where cities still stand…

The analog BUZZES.

DJ turns it off.

The stereo plays something that wasn't there when they listened before:

RECORDING but there are no pictures of that.

Shocked, DJ turns off the red light. They rewind the tape & listen again.

RECORDING i've made a name for myself, pulling our mast through the marbled fog—the lighthouse toppled over a year back, when children came from the outskirts, their only possessions hanging from their necks. they came to frame its fall. afterwards, back in their homes, they put pictures in cut-out squares of cardboard & hung them along hallways. each home offers one snap in the series. to get the scene, you'd have to walk through the town, house to house, to see it. most just look at the last one, when the thing had settled. i heard some hung from the deck, their feet dangling over the rocks & water. at night, the bridge blinks at us from its stretch through the black horizon, lights coursing across it. below, ships caught in the current grope through the water till they slam into the pilings or cliffsides. sometimes, sailors will rise from the waves. we've found their treasures in the sand, waterlogged books & hats, trinkets from the other places, where cities still stand. But there are no pictures of that…

The analog BUZZES. DJ waits.

The stereo plays something that wasn't there on the last listen:

RECORDING but there are no pictures of that.

dear survivors,

through the windows of the terminal we watch the fire gnaw at what's flammable. it surrounds us & we huddle in the space, cramped & sweating from the temperature. when the wind comes the terminal sways—its softened metal bends, creases. the flames disperse & at the crest where the town ends, we can see soldiers falling in the blowing blades & stalks of grass.

dear survivors,

i don't want to set a scene. after all, it's been done & you've seen other cities in this state, but it must be done. there are different smells & noises scratching through the landscape. you'd think that all the animals would have followed the fall, but only some have perished & only a few have trailed the exodus. there are still creatures coursing through the muscles of what's left, not hungry or rabid, but looking for a place to rest. they look at us with disinterest. a wolf does not scare, does not attack—it looks at us, bows its head, & climbs on a pile of concrete. we're here in the WRECKAGE, picking through piles. someone says, "two years ago, i kissed a woman here, & that night we stamped the pavement, telling stories about drugs & bad sex, till we went to her apartment & meshed our bodies together, laughing." now, it's only recognized by the street signs bent into the earth. "look at this," they say, "everything is ash & piles of bricks." & we can hear more WRECKAGE crossing the border & pummeling through another place.

dear survivors,

we've missed seconds, maybe minutes after the first blast, &
the WRECKAGE keeps circling like this, stealing time from us.
these jump cuts, gutted. for an hour it continues like this till
our bodies are dusted & slumped from turning over rocks
& kicking in what doors still stand. the survivors are few, &
they'd rather stay than follow us west. we leave them as the
night begins to seep. tonight, glowings pepper the other side
of the mountain range.

SCENE IX

A thick wood of evergreen. The sun is about to rise. The sky is bruise-blue. The night begins its rot into the orange of morning. SURVIVORS draw camp—

—a group of CHILDREN enter.

SURVIVORS do not speak. They wave the CHILDREN over.

From the edge of the WOOD'S CLEARING, the CHILDREN respond, keeping their distance.

> CHILDREN *(singing)*　this river we found
> we know it's full of pain
> there's a city near the good hills
> but we don't dare sing its name
> you must whisper its name
> when the wind is heavy
> you must whisper its name
> when the wind is heavy
> we want to tell you
> we want to tell you
> but there is no wind
> there is no wind
> we want to tell you
> we want to tell you
> but there is no wind
> there is no wind
> no wind
> no no—

dear survivors,

we think there are ghosts in the rubble. we can hear the ghostly sounds all night. we can hear something. we hear something. something is out there.

dear survivors,

there in the twilight we can hear the sound of coals turning to ash. when the tree line gets bluish & oh we will see the smoldering location.

this is not the last breath of an empire.

this is how a city feeds.

SCENE X

LEADER walks around his office. It is intact—the scene from earlier was just a vision. He keeps circling the office. The phone keeps ringing, but he ignores it. He keeps stopping at the window & looking. GENERAL walks in. He doesn't knock, just pushes through the door & walks up behind the LEADER. They don't speak for a good minute. LEADER turns & looks at him.

LEADER what's the status?

GENERAL someone is out there, taking them out.

LEADER we should contain that.

GENERAL i've had to send in reinforcements.

LEADER you need to know what's going on out there.

GENERAL it's bad. it's a new era.

LEADER no one can know what happened.

GENERAL i have no idea what you are referring to.

LEADER no one can know i was warned.

GENERAL i'm not sure i understand.

LEADER no one can know.

GENERAL have you heard of the city caspian?

LEADER's face goes cold. He trips back against the window.

GENERAL it exists?

LEADER does not answer.

GENERAL exits.

LEADER stares out the window. He turns around. The room is as it is. Still. He sighs. Sits at his desk.

Suddenly, the room splits open & a MASSIVE SHAFT OF LIGHT cuts through to the floor. AIDES & ADVISORS enter, but they are not dressed in suits & work clothes. We can see their wings. They gather in front of the desks.

AIDES & ADVISORS god has let go, what do you say now?

LEADER looks up at them, almost defiant. He is very careful about what he says in terms of fault, so he just looks.

AIDES & ADVISORS god has let go, will you listen now?

LEADER you couldn't stop it coming, what will convince me that you have the power to stop it where it is?

AIDES & ADVISORS we're not the ones setting fires.

LEADER you're not answering my questions.

AIDES & ADVISORS we cannot hear you over the flames.

LEADER your hyperbole is insulting.

AIDES & ADVISORS we can stop the *natural disaster* because we started it.

LEADER don't placate me.

AIDES & ADVISORS you let these people down, you made this happen, & we need you to listen to us. you, not them.

LEADER you punish the weak to get my attention.

AIDES & ADVISORS nothing gets your attention. the deaths are on you & you know this & you set these fires because you know this, so you may not be listening, but your action shows that you are aware of what you've done, or failed to do. more are dying, more will die. *(pause, dramatically. LEADER goes to speak sometime in the silence, but they continue, starting again before he can pontificate excuses.)* so we need to know if you're ready to listen.

LEADER will you put things back to the way they were?

AIDES & ADVISORS you must see the WRECKAGE.

LEADER the WRECKAGE will end & no one will know.

VOICE *(from the shaft of light)* caspian.

LEADER no.

VOICE caspian.

LEADER don't.

AIDES & ADVISORS we have not touched caspian, your soldiers will not. caspian is out there & someone will find it & you will be known.

LEADER no one will find it.

AIDES & ADVISORS what will make you listen?

LEADER get out.

VOICE the gates have opened.

LEADER no.

VOICE the gates have opened.

LEADER stop it.

VOICE caspian is calling. the gates have opened.

AIDES & ADVISORS the gates have opened.

LEADER stop it. get out.

LEADER covers his ears. Childishly, he moves around the office, making blah-blah-blah-blah *noises at the top of his lungs.*

VOICE & AIDES & ADVISORS continue.

The MASSIVE SHAFT OF LIGHT mutates into different colors till it turns dark, blood red. AIDES & ADVISORS let their wings FLAP.

LEADER continues blah-blah-blah-blah*ing.*

VOICE caspian is calling. the gates have opened.

AIDES & ADVISORS the gates have opened.

VOICE caspian is calling. the gates have opened.

AIDES & ADVISORS the gates have opened.

VOICE caspian is calling. the gates have opened.

AIDES & ADVISORS the gates have opened.

VOICE caspian is calling. the gates have opened.

AIDES & ADVISORS the gates have opened.

VOICE caspian is calling. the gates have opened.

AIDES & ADVISORS the gates have opened.

VOICE caspian is calling. the gates have opened.

AIDES & ADVISORS the gates have opened.

VOICE caspian is calling. the gates have opened.

AIDES & ADVISORS the gates have opened.

VOICE caspian is calling. the gates have opened.

AIDES & ADVISORS the gates have opened.

VOICE caspian is calling. the gates have opened.

AIDES & ADVISORS the gates have opened.

VOICE caspian is calling. the gates have opened.

AIDES & ADVISORS the gates have opened.

VOICE caspian is calling. the gates have opened.

AIDES & ADVISORS the gates have opened.

VOICE caspian is calling. the gates have opened.

AIDES & ADVISORS the gates have opened.

VOICE caspian is calling. the gates have opened.

AIDES & ADVISORS the gates have opened.

VOICE caspian is calling. the gates have opened.

AIDES & ADVISORS the gates have opened.

VOICE caspian is calling. the gates have opened.

AIDES & ADVISORS the gates have opened.

VOICE caspian is calling. the gates have opened.

AIDES & ADVISORS the gates have opened.

VOICE caspian is calling. the gates have opened.

AIDES & ADVISORS the gates have opened.

VOICE caspian is calling. the gates have opened.

AIDES & ADVISORS the gates have opened.

VOICE caspian is calling. the gates have opened.

AIDES & ADVISORS the gates have opened.

VOICE caspian is calling. the gates have opened.

AIDES & ADVISORS the gates have opened.

VOICE caspian is calling. the gates have opened.

AIDES & ADVISORS the gates have opened.

VOICE caspian is calling. the gates have opened.

AIDES & ADVISORS the gates have opened.

VOICE caspian is calling. the gates have opened.

AIDES & ADVISORS the gates have opened.

VOICE caspian is calling. the gates have opened.

AIDES & ADVISORS the gates have opened.

dear survivors,

when the city was out of view, we heard the destruction, & hours later, we smelled the burning. the next day, we backtracked to look for survivors. there were none, so we left, trailing cautiously. we found a river that had not filled with ash & debris. it was clear as ever, it was pure. we followed it to another, just as clean. we did not have to cook what water we had gathered in our canteens. it's as though someone had filtered the trash & sewage from the water. today, when the river folks, it's filled with evidence. the hope we felt days ago vanishes. now, we avoid rivers as much as we can, we talk about what rivers might look like now.

dear survivors,

heat comes quick today, first time in months. it comes & we strip our clothes till we're in our underwear, sweating. the fires thrive & we have to put them out, one by one. hours in, our bodies are smeared black & gray, but there are not fires anywhere. the heat passes suddenly, & we are shoving ourselves back into our pants & coats. then the rain comes, forcing us to find cover somewhere in a cavernous pile of the WRECKAGE, where half of an old college cafeteria still stands. BECKER HALL a sign says. we find a few cans of peaches & old soda cans.

dear survivors,

the hills are sepia in smog-light. in the valley, there are no
ghosts, but the locals have claimed so for years. they say there
are only shadows moving along the ground, not bodies. we
witness this miracle. only days later, on the ridge, we see the
source. there are feral children down there, stalking around
for food—they've lived down there for years, before the
WRECKAGE, now they are free. we've heard people talking
about ghosts & how they make dead soldiers. we're not
interested in justice or the intentions of the spiritual. we just
wanted our homes to stand through this, but the shaking
came & pried our walls apart, tore our roof from its place,
lifted foundation from the ground. the fire worked its
way around the house & crawled through the back half of
town, sending survivors into the river to wait it out. when it
got quiet at the water, the other survivors didn't even bother
to rummage through what the fire left. two days later, there
are dead soldiers scattered in the meadows above the city. we
do not look through their belongings. the other survivors
have been talking about their dreams, about a city in the
west, about heading there.

SCENE [ ]

In a lighthouse.

Tall, reaching through the fog—or is it smoke—its spire bent from the wind.

SURVIVORS watch the water below. Its waves, they tumble like buildings. This body of water is large. The fog is so thick it's hard to see if there's land on the other side of the water. Waves crash & crash into the shore.

There is debris of the WRECKAGE *in the sea—the cliff-side cities collapsed into the water, the boats capsized in the waves, & bodies now float on the surface.*

The waves deliver evidence of the WRECKAGE.

SURVIVOR boats have all capsized.

SURVIVOR hope is difficult when the waves look like that.

SURVIVOR reality is more prudent anyway.

SURVIVOR reliable, you mean.

SURVIVOR no, prudent. reliable no longer means—

dear survivors,

in a lighthouse, we're casting shadows, all flashlights, & in the stairwell's creak, through the blur of dirty glass, we hear it outside. not cicadas, nor the sound of what's still banging around, settling. there are no survivors, just a couple of squirrels.

SCENE XI

TIME — DUSK (OR SOMETIME WHERE THE LIGHT LOOKS LIKE IT'S
FILTERED THROUGH A DARK, WET CLOTH)

SPOTLIGHT CENTER STAGE reveals a town leveled. Just WRECKAGE.
*Just toppled buildings & caved-in roads. There is glass & concrete &
brick & drywall & wires & plastic & metal & pieces & pieces & pieces
of civilization in heaps, scattered like post-tantrum.*

*A group of SOLDIERS standing in front of a group of SURVIVORS.
Our SURVIVORS.*

*Some SOLDIERS are pouring gasoline & other flammable materials on
everything they can see. Two of them are discussing & pointing into the*
WRECKAGE, *mapping the plot of the prospective fire. We cannot hear them,
but it's clear what they are doing.*

One SOLDIER addresses the SURVIVORS:

> SOLDIER *(yelling commands)* pry yourself from the wall's
> touch & give your name when asked.

*ACROSS THE STAGE the red light BUZZES, desk lamp switches on,
DJ speaks over the action.*

*SOLDIERS yell, continue dousing. We can only hear the sound of the
dousing. But they are yelling. We can see them yelling, but we can't hear
them over that sound & the DJ.*

> DJ see, the scene got royal in its sorrow, turning sharp-
> toothed & confetti-wet, till our leaders were kneeling, hands
> clasped, pleading. after the flags came down, the sky-line
> went bare & the tops of buildings still. in white rooms, they
> piled in, making demands about what they should be raised
> to wave for. & here, in the strangled-light of the alley behind
> what used to be *the* bar, evening has hit its brakes, & we're
> all howling & sober, & out at the edges of towns, the wind
> kicked up, stripping trees bare.

The red light goes off. DJ switches off the desk lamp. Disappears in the dark.

SOLDIERS *(yelling, & we can totally hear them now—it's really loud)* tomorrow the sky will be revelation-gray, the roads will be slabs covered in ash, & the insides of the buildings will empty out, but you're still resisting.

Long pause.

A MASSIVE SHAFT OF LIGHT appears from the clouds, but within view of the SOLDIERS & SURVIVORS. It seems as though they can't see it, but they can feel *it. We can see it in their faces.*

VOICE *(from the shaft of light)* the gates have opened.

SOLDIERS so give your name.

SURVIVORS we have no names.

SOLDIERS we need your names.

SURVIVORS we no longer have names. you took them from us when you burnt the history from us. our names came from the past & you have kept that past from our future.

SOLDIERS ok. fair enough. fair enough. tell us, what did your names used to be?

SURVIVORS we no longer remember. you have taken our memories too.

SOLDIERS we are not gonna ask again.

SURVIVORS yes you will & our answers will be the same. we have no names. we are only survivors.

SOLDIERS *(grabbing the youngest of the SURVIVORS, shaking them)* give me your name, goddamnit!

SURVIVORS we have no names. you took them from us.

SOLDIERS forget them! it doesn't matter!

A flame rises behind them.

SOLDIERS let them burn or retreat.

A SOLDIER breaks formation. Speaks:

SOLDIER *(to the SURVIVORS, humanity creeping in)* Run! Run!

Everyone scatters OFFSTAGE.

The SOLDIERS move along the rising flame as if they know how it breathes.

dear survivors,

the spine of asphalt curls at clear-cuts, bordering the two-lanes. mountain-light strobes for hours through the cloud cover, streaking through the skeletons of trees. birds neck the branches. before there was worry, kids made up stories about monsters.

SCENE XII

TIME — OUTSIDE OF TIME

Time moves around the GHOSTS. Time passes as though projected on a white sheet, but it loops & repeats & rewinds & plays & plays. The GHOSTS seem to dance, seem to be dancing through time, occasionally their limbs reach through the barriers of time & out over the stage, then back outside of time.

ONSTAGE, SOLDIERS pass by – they look terrified, they're shaking. We hear the ghostly sounds entering time. These men coddle their weapons. Their terror rises.

Just OFFSTAGE, a city. Its WRECKAGE *has spilled onto the stage—glass, chunks of concrete, rebar, a car door.*

SOLDIERS sling their weapons over their shoulders & start pouring gasoline on the WRECKAGE. *Many of the SOLDIERS walk OFFSTAGE. But we can hear the GLUG GLUG GLUG of gasoline.*

The GHOSTS reach their limbs back into time. They touch each SOLDIER on their appendages. One by one. The SOLDIERS fall in a line. Then OFFSTAGE we hear SOLDIERS dropping. Gasoline spills onto the stage.

The GHOSTS continue their dancing. They begin to sing, sort of:

GHOSTS your mind is a trench,

became one a year ago,

when the empire began its struggle

to stay afloat,

and the outsiders left their vessels,

climbed the walls,

and stood pigeon-toed at the top

269

of the wall.

no longer the conquered people

gritting their teeth

at those who ruled,

no longer regretting the voice

they cover, no longer skirting

the borders along the tree line.

this time they were seen & heard,

and years later,

we would sing about them,

stories where the narratives

gave these people names & histories,

things we never had the chance

to ask about.

SPOTLIGHT UPSTAGE reveals another pile of dead SOLDIERS.

The SOUND OF TRUMPETS playing scales, a PIANO accompanies. Arpeggios dissect & are fed back into themselves, occasionally the leftover notes move in and out of key, as though slipping—

GHOSTS do you hear that?

those scales?

that piano & trumpet

the key of c

that piano & trumpet

the key of c

that piano & trumpet

the key of c

that piano & trumpet

the key of c

that piano & trumpet

the key of c

that piano & trumpet

the key of c

that piano & trumpet

the key of c

those scales—

those scales—

those scales—

those scales—

the key of c?

the gates have opened the gates have opened the gates have
opened the gates have opened the gates have opened the
gates have opened the gates have opened the gates have
opened the gates have opened the gates have opened the

gates have opened the gates have opened the gates have
opened the gates have opened the gates have opened the
gates have opened the gates have opened the gates have
opened the gates have opened the gates have opened the
gates have opened the gates have opened the gates have
opened the gates have opened the gates have opened the
gates have opened the gates have opened the gates have
opened the gates have opened the gates have opened the
gates have opened the gates have opened the gates have
opened the gates have opened the gates have opened

the gates have opened

but not for you

not for you not for you not for you not for you not for you
not for you
            not for you
                    not for you
                            not for you
                not for you
                        not for you
not for you
not for you
not for you
not for you
not for you
not for you
not for you
not for you.

dear survivors,

the ghost rebellion wasn't organized. but it was nightly, &
silent. foxes weren't aware. only humans. we find bodies
outside, charred. we never see the murderers in action, but
murder happens.

locals have their stories—it's ghosts making them pay.

adults whisper to children & peer through the syrup-night.
"look," they say, "you can see them in the woods. you can
see them hatching plans. they'll protect us if the soldiers
come. if we sacrifice. if we take it that far."

dear survivors,

our hope evaporates when we come off the ridge. the city
is a trembling fire. looks like popcorn of concrete & glass.
we watch till it's certain we've seen enough & retreat to the
forest for the night. the soldiers move with the wind, the
fire-light is drastic in its shape, & the air is clotted.

dear survivors,

we lost our breaths when the elevation leveled. the buildings were leftovers, as though a canyon had emptied itself. this isn't a joke or some half-cocked prophecy spilling from the page bound in leather, but a snapshot after the WRECKAGE had settled & the fire quit. & now, there's nothing for us to arrive at. our anger rises. what are we even doing? this is not about the way travelers slow at the mid-way. this is about the splaying where cities used to hunch. in the aftermath, they tied terror to the landscape. in each place, the names of old kings were once ballasts, now they are shattered & left to sift through.

SCENE H

dear survivors,

when the gun went off, fired into the wall behind us, we didn't flinch or cower. at this point, we had accepted that what would kill us would find us when it was time, but when the shell hit the ground, the boy who left the safety off & slipped his finger over the trigger called our names. we ignored him & carried ourselves inside.

INTERMISSION

The theatre HOUSE LIGHTS UP. Intermission starts, with the curtain still parted. Slowly, ACTORS all gather on stage. They are waiting for the second act. They have stripped out of their costumes.

They are glowing.

They are drinking.

They are laughing.

They are clearly drunk.

They raise their bottles to the heavens.

They raise their eyes.

They begin to sing, hymn-like:

> ACTORS this one's for the kids
>
> who didn't make the cut.
>
> look how the bottle's been dry for hours
>
> & everyone's one step away from
>
> giving up the ghost, except for the ones
>
> in the corner who took up praying
>
> at sunday dinner. they speak
>
> across tables & rooms as though
>
> they're introducing colors to the dark
>
> or guitar twang to silence.

They drink in gulps. They raise their bottles again to the heavens.

ACTORS this one's for the kids

who talked successful skin

& the smooth surfaces of photographs

or water on fresh concrete—this before

babies with high school heroes,

made in back of cars, at basement parties,

or bathrooms of bars.

robbed of their old conversations,

of their sleek young bodies.

it's not the bodies they miss,

but the silence of being single at night,

when all that's heard is a lover's snore,

or what's blowing outside.

now in the silence, they listen for their babies,

they listen for death foot-stepping in the room,

she's always curious around cribs.

They drink in gulps. They raise their bottles again to the heavens.

ACTORS this one's for the women

singing battle hymns

in the bloodied fog of dawn.

they're at it, unaware of what's coming.

their bodies have become machines who rise

& fall with the sun.

the melody flattens when the sun peeks

through & the fog becomes a curtain.

They drink in gulps. They raise their bottles again to the heavens.

ACTORS this one's for the crowd

settling at the edge of the storm, while peddlers

toe up to open windows with palms full,

leave with fists full. the body's there,

curled up & cold. the parents are headed out,

from the way-back of town, panic thickening

when they see the crowd. in the woods,

lovers once fled from murders, from the scene,

& into the storm. if chase were given,

someone would surely gain. only here,

it's not the law that follows, it's guilt.

They drink in gulps. They raise their bottles again to the heavens.

ACTORS this one's for all the kids

who want to be cowboys.

EVERYONE *shouts* **YES!**

      ACTORS & they'd buy a pistol to spin the chamber late

      at night, just 'cause it sounds cool, that click

      & clicking, & it makes them look

      like real men with real power—

      makes them feel like real men

      that thick fucking handshake deep in their palms—

They drink in gulps. They raise their bottles again to the heavens.

      ACTORS this one's for all the women

      ascending, you know,

      the ones who start dropping down the hill,

      as if they could vanish in the silence of curves

      before the straight lines of the city, its arms open,

      ready to suffocate what's expendable

      & keep what it can use. look, birds gather

      like a choir on rooftops looking in windows

      at lovers over sheets—the tv glare rubbing

      itself against the skin—

      & these pastures start humming remnants of hymns

      about what it means to go *west*.

They drink in gulps. They raise their bottles again to the heavens.

ACTORS this one's for the kids

mouthing off to the deputy

when he comes around for questioning.

someone saw the thing go down?

the girl had only found blood.

if someone had, they would've

seen one of the shooters

cringe at the touch of the barrel against

his skin when he tucked it, still hot, into his pants.

years later, his part-time lover will trace

his body to stop on it. when asked,

he'll recall the story, but only tell it as though

he's a hero saving girls from boys full

of lust & thirst. this happens in a motel

when he's thirty-two & still trying

to unhook himself

from the choice that claimed his twenties.

They drink in gulps. They raise their bottles again to the heavens.

ACTORS this one's for the kids

making calls for the future king.

decked out in leather & corduroy they hang

in phone booths listening to dial

tones & constant ringing.

EVERYONE _shouts_ **NO!**

the calls don't come from the hills

& canyons of the city, but spread from

an echo inside a cave north of missouri,

& before it reaches where it should,

all wet & heavy,

it turns into a steady bass note quivering

through the plains, over rivers,

up into tree branches & rooftops.

They drink in gulps. They raise their bottles again to the heavens.

ACTORS this one's for the kids

left from the wives of frontier men,

the ones settled & tired. these kids only know

what lies inside the four corners of borders.

the range packs them in & only a few think

to ask what's in the dirt outside

where the horizon slacks. the answers

come out rusted & aged, centered in folklore

the town made back

when the woods still spoke to them.

They drink in gulps. They raise their bottles again to the heavens.

ACTORS this one's for the men

who lost livestock

when the kids from iowa city burned the livery,

'cause they hated the way it looked,

all rusted & chipped.

"better not be misremembering where you're from!"

one of the boys screamed after the fire was set.

to escape, they slipped down the river in the weight

of the night. the water carries them, loosens them

from their sins, peels the city right off,

trading asphalt & glass

for the skeletons of the ghost woods.

when they wake, they are surrounded by trees

& dark thick as soil. one says,

"where are we?" then, the wolves start in.

The toast is over. They continue to drink. Continue to laugh.

Two ACTORS move from the crowd out to the front of the stage.

They dialogue:

> ACTOR yeah, we've all got our own versions of drunken-mouthed loyalty, & we'll tear at its meaning till—
>
> ACTOR there's no lid to twist.
>
> ACTOR the city gave them reasons to let go the columns.
>
> ACTOR the wind knocked the bell around in the tower, opened windows, & carried fire from the river's skin from building to building.
>
> ACTOR it's not déjà vu, it has happened before, back when men left the first WRECKAGE to settle.
>
> ACTOR we wanted mercy to grow a neck, so it could turn its head & see the stampede carry from the city's chin.
>
> ACTOR the nails keep shuffling the turnarounds till wind takes a breather, but the damage is done, & getting done, & some have laid claim to brick & two-story towers of glass & concrete.
>
> ACTORS dear brothers, dear sisters, dear survivors: listen, please, we've been warning everyone for years.

The STAGE LIGHTS UP—all ACTORS have gathered behind them. They stand in mock-prayer stance, looking up.

> ACTORS dear brothers, dear sisters, dear survivors. dear brothers, dear sisters, dear survivors. dear brothers, dear sisters, dear survivors. dear brothers, dear sisters, dear survivors. dear brothers, dear sisters, dear survivors. *(short pause to take breaths)* the narrative is yours. the narrative is yours. the narrative is yours. the narrative is yours. the narrative is yours. the narrative. the narrative. the narrative.

dear survivors,

we made our way to the coast & among the stacks of rubble
we find a still-standing building of white concrete & metal.
were we followed? it's not clear. soldiers emerge from behind
us, their weapons clinking together, the smell of gasoline.
one soldier looks at the building, "it won't burn. one of you
needs to open the door for us." we try to explain, but they
line us against the wall, ash rising up our legs. gunshots crack
somewhere from the stacks & the soldiers collapse, blood &
insides scatter the ground. the door opens, we are let inside.

dear survivors,

from our sleep we can hear the word *caspian*. in the morning, everyone denies it. someone says, "it must've been the wind."

SCENE XIII

Cul-de-sac. The city smokes in the background. The towers are bent & fallen. The skyline looks like broken teeth or a mountain range split apart.

A group of SURVIVORS stands on the porch.

SURVIVORS enter from OFFSTAGE & walk towards the porch. The sound of WRECKAGE *everywhere.*

They speak to each other but we cannot hear them over the sound of WRECKAGE.

The meeting is tense, but soon it calms down as the sound of WRECKAGE *revs—then suddenly it stops.*

SURVIVOR you have seen soldiers.

SURVIVOR it's just us out here. when things got real bad, we started draping blankets over the front windows of our house. the morning benders had begun on a friday & kept at it till midweek, when the sun crept in from the corner of the window & spread across the room, reminding us of work & family obligations. but none of us could peel ourselves from the house, so we flipped coins for exits. neighborhood kids figured out what we were up to in the front room, started banging sticks against trash cans & fencing, hence the blankets. we ignored the noises & knocks at the door, as we could allow no visitors to interrupt our work. when it was over, we told ourselves we would toast the outcome, congratulate our work, & sleep, but in the midst of this, some would have to crawl to the kitchen for popsicles or a can of tuna, some gave into the hours & shot-eyes, while the rest of us carried on, letting our ribs absorb our skin.

SURVIVOR any help you can provide—we are traveling.

SURVIVOR help is a waste—we're futile.

SURVIVOR we are following the WRECKAGE. following the fires. we will find answers & we will find safety.

SURVIVOR then you have heard of caspian.

SURVIVOR is that a question? what is caspian?

SURVIVOR the city of caspian lies flat between two hills, plumped & wooded, flat-lining the horizon suddenly, as though god has pulled the cord from the wall.

dear survivors,

we find our way out of the city. there's a figure plucking through the bodies. we see her from the ridge, but when we get down in the meadow & tread through the tall grass, she's gone. just birds pecking the faces & exposed limbs. the pockets are out-turned & this isn't the first we've seen of her. she leaves the smell of jasmine & cinnamon. someone mentions the lack of rats, mentions how the cities secrete them from every crease & pore, but since she's appeared there's been none. someone calls her the rat-catcher. we can't claim to have learned from the WRECKAGE after all the evidence we found only covered what we already knew, complicated the whole story. & above the interstate, where protestors hang signs from the overpass, someone had draped flags over the rail & chain-link. these weren't from nations, but handmade—you know the kind, you know they don't really mean anything. they're just ideas. & today, we read the words out loud, & repeat till we're a half-mile north, colliding.

dear survivors,

in the pines & cedars we give chase. only one soldier left
after the ghost-killings & he's sobbing. his gun jammed
when he tried to fire on us, so he dropped it & ran. we hear
him crunching & crying through the forest, & in a clearing,
he spins around & shouts "what do you want?" we want to
know why he's setting fires. "orders," he says, then asks us
why we killed his platoon. we tell him that we didn't. we
tell him ghosts don't like fires. his face turns still & wind
beats against his body. the weed tops slap his thighs & he
collapses. the wind retreats & ghost hair floats between us
& the body. we know what this means. we know there's no
need to check his pulse.

SCENE XIV

TIME — OUTSIDE OF TIME

Time moves around the GHOSTS. Time passes as though projected on a white sheet, but it loops & repeats & rewinds & plays & plays. The GHOSTS seem to dance, seem to be dancing through time, occasionally their limbs reach through the barriers of time & out over the stage, then back outside of time.

ONSTAGE a SOLDIER sprints across the stage. We hear the ghostly sounds entering time.

Our SURVIVORS enter from where the SOLDIER ran. They stand at the ENTRANCE OF THE STAGE.

The GHOSTS reach their arms back into time.

Our SURVIVORS watch as the SOLDIER goes limp. Falls.

The GHOSTS continue their dancing.

SPOTLIGHT UPSTAGE reveals a group of dead SOLDIERS in our time, lying in a row as though someone has laid them that way, all across the front of the stage.

The GHOSTS begin to sing, sort of.

Our SURVIVORS disappear, backing OFFSTAGE.

GHOSTS you can hear us now—

you can feel our wrath—

you can feel us taking swings—

keep swinging, we will keep swinging—

we are not done.

the gates have opened. the gates have opened. the gates have opened. the gates have opened. the gates have opened. the gates have opened. the gates have opened.

the gates have opened.

you can hear its sound—

the gates have opened.

you can hear its sound—

the gates have opened.

dear survivors,

along the way, we talk about what used to be. but that's history. now, all of these places are tombs or mounds of useless materials. we hate to do it, because it's become an hourly thing, but we make stories. the WRECKAGE gets filled with them. sometimes, we give bodies names. sometimes, we give them families.

dear survivors,

the soldiers get spooked & we wander right into the scattershot. their radios crackle with ghost-sightings.

SCENE XV

SURVIVORS spring onto the stage. A SOLDIER enters from the other side at a dead sprint. He stops, looking at the SURVIVORS. He turns & runs DOWNSTAGE, but stops. Sees something out in the AUDIENCE. He starts backing up. He looks back at the SURVIVORS.

SOLDIER i didn't do anything.

SURVIVORS it's not us.

GHOSTS *(we cannot see them but they are there, somewhere outside of time, sort of hovering around. we see an occasional ghost-limb enter time. we can hear them, attempting to enter our timeline.)* why do you keep burning & killing?

SOLDIER *(hearing the GHOSTS, looking wildly, pleading to the SURVIVORS)* please. please.

SURVIVORS it's not us.

GHOSTS you kill our memories, you kill our homes, & you kill us, the ones hiding, the ones who didn't flee or the ones stuck in the building, the ones forgotten, you burnt us into our histories.

SOLDIER orders. the fires are orders. we are following orders.

GHOSTS sometimes orders are wrong. you know they're wrong, but you smell of gasoline & smoke & rubble & you smell of our deaths.

SOLDIER i am not to blame.

GHOSTS we are all to blame, but you are the ones who have to feel the consequences, you are the ones who will become the trophies, the evidence of retaliation. your leader, we will find him somewhere in time & he will get what he will get. we

cannot find him. we will. one of you knows where he is &
one of you will lead us to him.

SOLDIER we are just soldiers.

GHOSTS you know more than you know.

SOLDIER we are just soldiers.

GHOSTS you know more than you know.

SOLDIER we are just survivors.

*An ETHEREAL WAIL. The SOLDIER collapses to the ground. The
SURVIVORS are still watching. It is clear the GHOSTS are gone.
SURVIVORS walk over & check the SOLDIER.*

SURVIVORS *(say something, but we cannot hear them, but it
is most likely bleak, filled with conflict—maybe it's something
nasty about the death of the SOLDIER. but there is something
truly broken in that face & the words are spoken softly, it must
come from a place of empathy or fear or exhaustion.)*

dear survivors,

i'm not certain if those sparks we caught curling up over
the hill were loose pieces of weather or the taut end of the
WRECKAGE, but it doesn't matter, 'cause our focus changes
when we get up there. someone built a dam & flooded the
lowlands. there are children on roofs & parents wading,
swimming from high-point to high-point, whether they're
cars, rocks, or even the tall part of a swing set. most of them
are working their way out to the bend leading out of town.
our road is high enough, so we watch them. as we gut the
highway—& below, the children keep waiting—the last
i see of them is rear-viewed & i think they're laughing at
jokes. if the empire knows of these incidents, they haven't
showed concern, & last anyone heard, there's barely a stir in
the capitol. maybe news will spread to them once it crosses a
river, swollen. someone tells us that what she's heard is that
the capitol is still standing, that the destruction skipped it
over.

The SOFT DIM LIGHT slowly lights the back corner of the stage. The red light BUZZES on. DJ speaks into the microphone.

> DJ to make it out, you must let time ferment & sway, you'll find air at the entrance. you must also insert yourself into the ranks of the forgotten. you must raise your voice in the sludge of darkness, your hands through it, as though you could dig yourself out. you can, & at the bottom you'll find light. you will find the pin-holed exit.

DJ rises & walks to the bookcase. They pick off a notebook, open & read. They read for a few minutes, then walk back to the microphone & begin again.

> DJ none of you have asked forgiveness—grace is conditional, i do not know where you would've heard otherwise. wrath can growl if it's let. it will devour till it quits, till it's satisfied, hunger met. once we let go, it unlatches from our control. this is your warning. revolt, to change things. *(pause)* i cannot introduce the soldiers without introducing its beginning. the world didn't just give up & start crumbling the cities man built. there were signs, whispers, & finally a warning. this is what happens when gods let go. those responsible saw the future, saw what would happen if they let go, felt the tremors in their rooms. they were warned. i must repeat this: they were warned. & those warnings were heard if not in real time, then through the passing of stories, & so when the WRECKAGE began, the ones responsible needed its evidence to vanish. this is where the soldiers come in. it started somewhere up near where the northern states border the atlantic, & it dozed south. months into the whole thing people started talking about caspian. but if there were a caspian, the soldiers would've heard & found it. they made it west. they didn't crisscross. & across interstates used to pump. & because everyone you see will utter this, you will wake with a word on your tongue:
> ### *caspian*.
> dream of giant gates spreading open, trumpets playing drawn out notes, harmonies backing. you will wake in the

damp morning. someone's preaching about caspian again over there, a half-jaunt through the woods, on the other side of the stream, there are soldiers talking. there are not crows squawking at each other in the morning. just the quiet chirping from nests & the sounds of a stream. listen: you can hear the ghost hair streaking through the fields. you can hear the ghosts behind the tree line searching for soldiers. you can hear the soldiers dying. you can hear the fires going. you can hear the WRECKAGE digging in. don't you know there isn't a *this* out there—find a place to dig in, make your own caspian. there's no reason to break your backs looking for something that's not even there.

dear survivors,

in the sudden vapor-light of dawn, these locals watch the travelers retreat, each step trespasses & quakes, & those too defeated or broken to carry themselves back the way they came join the collection & find themselves jobs. we look north daily, waiting for news to trickle down, we wonder if they're speaking our names. the blackest of birds gave up the wires & ends of branches, started perching next to us, watching—

dear survivors,

this rat-catcher burrowed through the collection of bodies
the soldiers left. the wind-up bird whistled from its cage,
while the retreaters kept still, & all the baby lotteries ceased
to function, & hangovers crept ahead, rolling through the
dead action, looking for passengers.

dear survivors,

look, the fires have quit & the engines work. we collapse
when it squeals, no chance to regroup, our intelligence soft,
sulfur, & lifts from its place, & we cannot pry ourselves
from the discarded carpet, cannot straighten up, unsteady.

TIME — LATE MORNING

A church, leveled—just its door frames & half of its brick walls stand. Around it, the town has been reduced to mounds of rubble.

A PREACHER makes piles of rubble from his church-pieces. A shovel, digging in. There are no SURVIVORS around him. If you look close you can see bodies under the WRECKAGE—*limbs, blood, whole bodies.*

A group of CHILDREN enters & pass—filthy, clothes torn & stained. They hum some tune with no words. The melody is familiar, but we do not know it.

PREACHER puts his shovel down.

> PREACHER where are your parents?

The CHILDREN do not speak. They continue.

> PREACHER where are your parents—this is no time for wandering.

> CHILDREN *(singing)* we have no parents
>
> we have no home
>
> we're searching for *(whispers)* caspian
>
> we're locked out till we're grown

> PREACHER let me help you.

> CHILDREN *(singing)* we need no help
>
> from silly preacher men
>
> we're on our own
>
> nothing you have is better than sin

PREACHER begins to follow them. He wants to help them. He believes he can, but they keep walking & he keeps following, across the stage till they disappear in the OFFSTAGE & he stops at the edge looking out— afraid to exit. He does not know what exists past the curtain.

PREACHER please come with me. i can help you.

CHILDREN your home is a pile of rocks

      god didn't save it

      ba ba ba baaaaaaaa

      ba ba ba baaaaaaaa

PREACHER let me help you.

CHILDREN *(singing)* you can't even help yourself

      you can't even help your flock

      we see those bodies

      it's easier to mock you

      than to listen to your cries

      ba ba ba baaaaaaaaaaaaaaaaaa

dear survivors,

the town is wet with rainfall. the soldiers' tracks veer away from the valley-mouth & head towards where the desert starts. the leaden heat slows us, but the rain keeps us cool. there is no fire to cross-out, just a town of wooden houses & water foul. ahead we find a carnage in the love trees—the ghosts have followed the soldiers at the border of the desert & taken their breaths.

SCENE XVIII

TIME — OUTSIDE OF TIME

Time moves around the GHOSTS. Time passes as though projected on a white sheet, but it loops & repeats & rewinds & plays & plays. GHOSTS seem to dance, seem to be dancing through time, occasionally their limbs reach through the barriers of time & out over the stage, then back outside of time.

GHOSTS continue their dancing. They begin to sing, sort of:

    GHOSTS hate breeds in dark places,

    where silence is the tires kicking

    down a dirt road after sundown,

    or the burning of wood,

    or the forest breathing.

    there's movement in there,

    the foxes & wolves speak to each other.

    this world is only half-known,

    halves of statuettes,

    shaded by the rocks in shapes of skyscrapers

    lining the horizon.

    survivors used to brag about how they faced

    east when the bombs when off.

    they got you dancing now?

    below the dead mountains,

spitting at the floors.

this is when they roll you.

when they get old they'll have

to answer to the empire.

they tried their best to keep

the distance safe, but fiction kept

pulling them back with turns of phrase

& a soft wind falling from the buildings.

dear survivors,

we'd always leave the soldiers for the rat-catcher. the leftovers of the fires sometimes only covered the previous WRECKAGE & the other way around. in those places, the fires didn't reach, sometimes, the WRECKAGE was invisible or never worked its way over the scene. orchards were rows of skeleton-frames, rotten fruit covering the dirt, the light-flutter sluggish in its reveal of the hordes of gashed buildings & homes.

dear survivors,

the air plucks salt from our bodies. the wind makes trees tambourine. the sun chaps the earth into crumbs. what splinters from crosses catch the wind rush from the valley's corner & carries into the bordered lawn, fencing those desert lives. outside, there is a mile-thick circumference of wood slats & stucco. i smell dirt & pomegranate. we camp just outside the debris. in the morning, the desert unlocks & lets us in, & ahead we see people rising from below the foundation.

SCENE XIX

TIME — EVENING

The moon glows like a lit orange.

SURVIVORS sit in the middle of a city, under a mountain.

There are fallen walls, loose limbs, & piles of glass—this city was big. It is now so leveled it looks like a massive salvage yard.

SURVIVORS huddle around a fire. They eat.

There's a throbbing pulse over the ridge's shoulder.

A rumble arrives, shakes the fire into smoke, kicks over their pots of food.

If we look closely in the dark, we can see a toppled city just beyond the fire.

> SURVIVOR this city used to be glass, & maybe it fell, but we've been thinking, maybe it lifted itself off the dirt & went upwards. either way, look, there are all these shards in the lawns, all over everything. the landscapes we know have become a fiction, borrowed objects & the quiet stance of stone, brushed with dirt & smears of wet, faded colors. feel the heat, it's descending every couple of hours, just enough to stop the frostbite from our appendages, just enough to lend some time, hours maybe. let us feel its cool corner tracing down our limbs, let it stop on our ankles, circle & carry back up.

> SURVIVOR *(as though quoting a poem)* the dance is imperative.

> SURVIVOR now our bodies are swollen, damp with the aftermath. your ease remains elusive, crossing & uncrossing legs, the way you shift your weight, sliding between the space where the door's not shutting. when the curse was cast, the bloodshed became foreign. we had no part in this, but our names were said. did you hear it pouring from the

survivors' teeth?

SURVIVOR you speak as though you're trying to write.

SURVIVOR you speak as though you can't see what's happening around us.

SURVIVOR you speak as though there is no god.

SURVIVOR you speak as though a fire does not kill.

SURVIVOR you speak as though this doesn't affect you & maybe it doesn't, maybe you'll see this through, but for us, this is everything, for us we feel this, & you can't take that from us you. what matters to us in our pain, it is ours. this loss is ours.

dear survivors,

in the dust, we found shelter underneath what used to be
an on-ramp. clearly other families had come & gone, or
maybe not families, but, together. someone had left a can of
corn. we dig in & eat, tired of the beans we'd been able to
ration for a good month. it's been a good year since we left
the city. all that asphalt, glass, & metal burying our travel,
hanging onto the echoes of life. we were of the lust to leave,
couldn't see the point in moving to a later place—could only
be worse, but the boys started showing up, then the roots,
& we'd wake, our bodies covered by both. so we shook off
what we could, fit what we could into our parents' vehicles,
& left down main street into the highways. the books &
films about this had cars & buses overturned, but the roads
were clean. nothing, as if a second coming took not humans
but worldly things. sure, there was a scrap of metal here &
there, but nothing more than remnants of trash. then the
dust storms came, taking away even that.

dear survivors,

the sun is choking the water out of us, burning holes in the roads & roofs. we kick through the desert till we get to the river before the pass. we fill our bottles & keep on. every four miles we take shade till our burns cool. & from the hood of shade we watch the sun work its fingers into the soil & blacktop. the road stretches its fingers through the high desert churning out paths. the difference between what you know about photographs & films & what they tell you mocks the space between you & the frame.

SCENE XX

TIME — EXPANSIVE

SPOTLIGHT moves from one space ONSTAGE to another as each character speaks.

The dialogue continues across the stage (nation) till they are all speaking at the same time & there is no SPOTLIGHT, just the STAGE LIGHTS at full blast—

—then as they coalesce into a wall of noise, SPOTLIGHT shines on the audience & everything goes silent & all we hear are the GHOSTS whispering—

THEN—

SPOTLIGHT with DJ in the red light.

SPOTLIGHT UPSTAGE LEFT. The SURVIVORS stand at the edge of a field, peering out from behind the tree line.

SPOTLIGHT

SPOTLIGHT

SPOTLIGHT

SPOTLIGHT

SPOTLIGHT

SPOTLIGHT follows the CHILDREN, GENERAL, PREACHER, AIDES & ADVISORS, SOLDIERS, LEADER, GHOSTS—this continues, the SPOTLIGHT going off & on, finding each character as they move off & on the stage. Some across distances, some in their same locations—pacing their office, standing in a radio booth, rebuilding their church—some outside of time, some in new places, doing new things—

—then they begin to speak, as this continues, as though they're speaking to each other, & I guess in a way they are. They just can't hear each other.

This **REPEATS & REPEATS & REPEATS**
(…as long as the director feels that it needs to)
(but i think it should be at least 3x, at least.)

DJ this place we/you seek is caspian.

SURVIVORS what is this place caspian?

GHOSTS caspian has all the answers.

SURVIVORS you have heard of caspian?

SURVIVORS you have heard of caspian—you must have.

CHILDREN *(singing)* caspian is a city where all the

> people go

> when the world is burning & the

> days grow

> cold caspian is a city where all the

> people go

> when the world is shaking & the

> cities unfold

SOLDIERS there are no maps to caspian, only whispers.

LEADER do not speak of caspian.

AIDES & ADVISORS *(singing)* caspian, caspian, caspian,
caspian, caspian, caspian,
caspian, caspian, caspian,
caspian, caspian, caspian,
caspian, caspian, caspian,
caspian, caspian, caspian,

316

                          caspian,   caspian,   caspian,
                          caspian,   caspian,   caspian,
                          caspian,   caspian,   caspian,
                          caspian,   caspian,   caspian,
                          caspian,   caspian,   caspian,

VOICE *(from the shaft of light)* you will pay for your sins!

SURVIVOR have you heard of caspian?

RAT-CATCHER *(singing)* on the path to caspian
                          these survivors arrive
                          & on the path to caspian
                          these soldiers all die—
                          doesn't matter who you are,
                          if your body ceases,
                          i will rob the riches
                          buried in the creases
                          of your clothes
                          of your bags
                          of your shoes
                          up on your head
                          on the path to caspian
                          my fortune awaits—

GHOSTS *(a very loud whisper—like they are trying to shout but can only whisper)* caspian, caspian, caspian, caspian, caspian, caspian. caspian, caspian, caspian, caspian, caspian, caspian. caspian, caspian, caspian, caspian, caspian, caspian. caspian, caspian, caspian, caspian, caspian, caspian.

SOLDIERS tell us, what is caspian, what is this place?

DJ this place we/you seek is caspian.

SURVIVORS what is this place caspian?

GHOSTS caspian has all the answers.

SURVIVORS you have heard of caspian?

317

SURVIVORS you have heard of caspian—you must have.

CHILDREN *(singing)* caspian is a city where all the

people go

when the world is burning & the

days grow

cold caspian is a city where all the

people go

when the world is shaking & the

cities unfold

SOLDIERS there are no maps to caspian, only whispers.

LEADER do not speak of caspian.

AIDES & ADVISORS *(singing)* caspian,   caspian,   caspian,
caspian,   caspian,   caspian,
caspian,   caspian,   caspian,
caspian,   caspian,   caspian,
caspian,   caspian,   caspian,
caspian,   caspian,   caspian,
caspian,   caspian,   caspian,
caspian,   caspian,   caspian,
caspian,   caspian,   caspian,
caspian,   caspian,   caspian,
caspian,   caspian,   caspian,

VOICE *(from the shaft of light)* you will pay for your sins!

SURVIVOR have you heard of caspian?

RAT-CATCHER *(singing)* on the path to caspian
these survivors arrive

& on the path to caspian
these soldiers all die—
doesn't matter who you are,
if your body ceases,
i will rob the riches
buried in the creases
of your clothes
of your bags
of your shoes
up on your head
on the path to caspian
my fortune awaits—

GHOSTS *(a very loud whisper—like they are trying to shout but can only whisper)* caspian, caspian, caspian, caspian, caspian, caspian. caspian, caspian, caspian, caspian, caspian, caspian. caspian, caspian, caspian, caspian, caspian, caspian. caspian, caspian, caspian, caspian, caspian, caspian.

SOLDIERS tell us, what is caspian, what is this place?

DJ this place we/you seek is caspian.

SURVIVORS what is this place caspian?

GHOSTS caspian has all the answers.

SURVIVORS you have heard of caspian?

SURVIVORS you have heard of caspian—you must have.

CHILDREN *(singing)* caspian is a city where all the

people go

when the world is burning & the

days grow

cold caspian is a city where all the

people go

when the world is shaking & the

cities unfold

SOLDIERS there are no maps to caspian, only whispers.

LEADER do not speak of caspian.

AIDES & ADVISORS *(singing)* caspian,   caspian,   caspian,
caspian,   caspian,   caspian,
caspian,   caspian,   caspian,
caspian,   caspian,   caspian,
caspian,   caspian,   caspian,
caspian,   caspian,   caspian,
caspian,   caspian,   caspian,
caspian,   caspian,   caspian,
caspian,   caspian,   caspian,
caspian,   caspian,   caspian,
caspian,   caspian,   caspian,

VOICE *(from the shaft of light)* you will pay for your sins!

SURVIVOR have you heard of caspian?

RAT-CATCHER *(singing)* on the path to caspian
these survivors arrive
& on the path to caspian
these soldiers all die—
doesn't matter who you are,
if your body ceases,
i will rob the riches
buried in the creases
of your clothes
of your bags
of your shoes
up on your head
on the path to caspian
my fortune awaits—

GHOSTS *(a very loud whisper—like they are trying to shout but can only whisper)* caspian, caspian, caspian, caspian, caspian, caspian. caspian, caspian, caspian, caspian, caspian, caspian. caspian, caspian, caspian, caspian, caspian, caspian. caspian, caspian, caspian, caspian, caspian, caspian.

SOLDIERS tell us, what is caspian, what is this place?

DJ this place we/you seek is caspian.

SURVIVORS what is this place caspian?

GHOSTS caspian has all the answers.

SURVIVORS you have heard of caspian?

SURVIVORS you have heard of caspian—you must have.

CHILDREN *(singing)* caspian is a city where all the

      people go

      when the world is burning & the

      days grow

      cold caspian is a city where all the

      people go

      when the world is shaking & the

      cities unfold

SOLDIERS there are no maps to caspian, only whispers.

LEADER do not speak of caspian.

AIDES & ADVISORS *(singing)* caspian, caspian, caspian,
                             caspian, caspian, caspian,

caspian, caspian, caspian,
caspian, caspian, caspian,
caspian, caspian, caspian,
caspian, caspian, caspian,
caspian, caspian, caspian,
caspian, caspian, caspian,
caspian, caspian, caspian,
caspian, caspian, caspian,
caspian, caspian, caspian,

VOICE *(from the shaft of light)* you will pay for your sins!

SURVIVOR have you heard of caspian?

RAT-CATCHER *(singing)* on the path to caspian
these survivors arrive
& on the path to caspian
these soldiers all die—
doesn't matter who you are,
if your body ceases,
i will rob the riches
buried in the creases
of your clothes
of your bags
of your shoes
up on your head
on the path to caspian
my fortune awaits—

GHOSTS *(a very loud whisper—like they are trying to shout but can only whisper)* caspian, caspian, caspian, caspian, caspian, caspian. caspian, caspian, caspian, caspian, caspian, caspian. caspian, caspian, caspian, caspian, caspian, caspian. caspian, caspian, caspian, caspian, caspian, caspian.

SOLDIERS tell us, what is caspian, what is this place?

> *When the REPETITION ENDS there's a LONG PAUSE—& **everyone turns to the** AUDIENCE— **waits** (…one two three…) then shouts:*

EVERYONE CAS-PI-AN! CAS-PI-AN! CAS-PI-AN!

dear survivors,

the half-gray dawn stays put. rain washed the cobble, & in our doorways, all that desert light unable to rise, we move through the surface. the WRECKAGE put a caesura in the pulse-beat of the moment. plucking the sun for our shoulders, everyone sings, our flagged skylines are no more—just shred cloth half-there, just flapping in the wind. one survivor says, "when the rumble came, the citizens fled northwest till they could toe the snow-line." now, this place, its basins of silt & light-flutter feels like whimpers.

dear survivors,

we find a notebook, leather & worn, sitting behind the bricks of a well. there are notes & notes about caspian. what is it? where is it? what to expect? we do not agree on its authenticity. but we keep it.

SCENE XXI

A thick wood. The sun plummeted & the orange & plum of sunset has darkened into a bruise across the horizon.

SURVIVORS enter & move through the wood & come upon a large clearing of tall grass & a small stream filled with rocks. When they are halfway across the clearing, about where the stream cuts through, a party of WOMEN enter the clearing.

The SURVIVORS wave.

The WOMEN scatter in pairs, back into the wood.

> SURVIVORS *(yelling as the WOMEN flee)* we mean no harm, we mean no harm! please!

The sounds of fleeing fill the theater from OFFSTAGE: branches CRACKING, footsteps THUDDING, then after a few moments, SILENCE.

They have not moved. They begin moving towards the other side.

> SURVIVORS *(shouting)* hello! *(long pause, silence. the SURVIVORS look at each other, peer into the woods. nothing. silence. an owl hoots. somewhere, a branch breaks in the far distance behind them that they don't even look. crickets or some kind of night-insect makes noise like little violins in the moonlight. wait.)* hello!

dear survivors,

so we begin collecting what we hear from others about this caspian. we cannot understand it, so we write & write & write every time we hear about caspian. sometimes, at night, we hear the word carried in the wind. sometimes, another survivor tells us about it. no one has been inside its gates, it is all word-of-mouth. no one knows the source of it, except that maybe the wind told them or they just woke up with this name on their lips, this idea in their brains. some of these we hear multiple times, some we only hear once.

caspian is not what you'd expect. there are halos floating overhead. no white robes watching from cloud covers.

it's just a city with buildings & people.

no gold inside.

walking the street's like flipping through a phone-book at midnight. but the doors only open if you're called.

it's a place in a story.

the gates only open if you're called.

you'll hear them [the gates] opening.

trumpets & pianos.

the city of caspian lies flat between two hills, plumped & wooded, flat-lining the horizon suddenly as though god has pulled the cord from the wall.

the kids there don't call themselves pilgrims, but outsiders.

all that lies inside are circles & degrees rounding off, back to where they started.

most never make it, end up settling with the out-siders in the scattered towns in the dips & valleys.

the only way inside the city is through the gates.

only handfuls ever see it.

many grow tired of waiting & retreat back to wherever they came from.

history isn't simple.

its history, it's full of the debris of salvation & chunks of what-was-left-of-faith-gone-wrong.

the difference between blood & bone marrow.

there is a cluster of crosses on a hill.

inside, faith has become a mouth, opening & closing & spitting out what enters.

since the first church laid its first brick, the dark one hasn't been seen inside.

before caspian's gates were risen, the dark one would be lurking around corners, smoking hand-rolled cigarettes & offering them to the younger ones, or tying shoelaces together at crosswalks.

when the gates went up, they pushed him out & so he went east towards cacti & arroyos, where shadows scamper under rocks & the fingers pet at the base of oaks.

between there & home are spaces. these spaces are border towns, not caspian, though maps mark them as such.

caspian waits behind the gates, where the churches seem to erect themselves daily.

pastors & priests give up what they had for the chance to make their own following. the hopefuls scour the roadside leading towards the gates for signs, clues, or pieces of maps to guide them.

the ones who've settled outside the gates wake to the slur of travelers passing through—or trying to.

SCENE XXII

SURVIVORS move across the stage—it is now a desert. Rocks & dried-up streams, now arroyos. They do not speak. They are walking towards a large tree & cluster of rocks STAGE LEFT.

Once there, they put down their materials. They drink water. They eat. They look out.

Behind them, somewhere OFFSTAGE, the sound of WRECKAGE *moves from right to left. They follow it with their gaze. They continue to rest. To drink. To eat.*

The RING of a church bell. Everyone stops. Looks towards it. They begin to grab their gear.

SURVIVOR that sounds like church bells.

SURVIVOR we're not close to caspian.

SURVIVOR you know no one knows where that is. maybe there are people there.

SURVIVOR everyone is packing.

SURVIVOR we have to see. what if there are people?

SURVIVOR we need to rest.

SURVIVOR we need to find people.

SURVIVOR we need to rest though. the people will be there in an hour if they're there now.

SURVIVOR you speak as if you know—you don't.

SURVIVOR we need rest.

The bells are still ringing.

Half of the SURVIVORS have their gear & materials ready to go. The other half have sat back down, clearly exhausted.

A SURVIVOR relaxes, slides off their backpack, & sits on the ground. They pull out an apple & begin to eat. Another SURVIVOR does the same.

SURVIVOR i'm glad those trees still had apples.

SURVIVOR i hope there are people there when we get there. i just want to see someone else. i just want to see that there are people making it out here. what are we even doing here? we just keep walking & walking. we just keep moving & doing what?

SURVIVOR we don't even know if there was anyone there though. we only hear bells, that doesn't prove anything.

The bells are still going.

SURVIVOR the bells are still going. we don't even know if caspian is real. we don't even know what it is.

SURVIVOR we don't, do we?

SURVIVOR where are we going?

SURVIVOR like we tell everyone, we're following the fires. but really we're waiting to learn if caspian is real.

SURVIVOR let's not lie to ourselves. we are just living till something unleashed kills us. there's probably no caspian, but we cling to it because it's some kind of pin-holed light at the end of a pitch-black tunnel.

SURVIVOR these apples are good.

Over the hills, a storm comes—rain first. Then thunder. Lightning.

The hills light up in the storm like a festival.

SURVIVORS watch the storm from under the tree.

dear survivors,

the storm left tide pools pocketing the road, & when the sunset goes red, it looks biblical, like pools of bloodshed, & back behind us dark has set. we keep in what's left of the light & scavenge the ruins, watch the lapsing fires behind us when we straighten up. this morning was dew-soaked, today was flyspecked & boiling, cities shimmering ahead of us, then no, the terminus came & went, open to us, in the blackened crags of the ranges around us, gray storm light bleaches the red of the west.

The SOFT DIM LIGHT slowly lights the back corner of the stage. The red light BUZZES on. DJ speaks into the microphone.

DJ there are churches. that's why it won't rumble or burn. people say this has been for years. these weren't always places of worship, & even now, there are no priests or rabbis, no teachers. these places were safe roofs & walls once inside the gates, but they grew altars & baptismals & pews. travelers flock to where they're called. before long, these shelters evolved into churches. it's simple, really. people needed faith. voices gathered, first in couplets, then quartets, & became a choir, violent in its vibration, sharp in its form, wide in its justification. but my god, caspian is a myth, something formed to give the desperate some hope, like god at a deathbed, god in a crashing plane. it's not there. we would know, we've been everywhere by now, twice. there isn't a town untouched by the aftermath—some still stand, out along the smallest of roads, but those couldn't survive the turning of weather or the absence of men & women. & people keep preaching, but when you hear this, know this is a lie: caspian is like heaven. just another place that will soon be nothing but a pile of rocks & glass & dust, but just like other new homes, this place is built on the religious staking claim with their stories of answers. & here i am to tell you what leaders have passed here in search of caspian & what they preach & believe, & what empty promises & teachings they share.

DJ stops and suddenly looks OFFSTAGE. They are dead-still, afraid. They wait. There is nothing there, but they want to be sure. So they wait & wait. When it is clear nothing is there, they lean back, real close to the microphone, & go.

DJ *(speaking quietly, but forcefully, as though they know this must be heard)* listen: when preachers grow tired of congregations full of sinners & faithless men & doubters, they seek caspian. droves of faithful. they hollow out buildings & preach what they know, what they feel, filling the seats one by one, every time the gates open. sunsets clear the streets of the wicked. they retreat to the churches still left for them, full of blood & bile, & the hopeless weight of all the *next times i'll do better*. the church fees take care of it. just pay your dues. you hear that? it's coming from down in the creases of the valley. really moving now, like cattle fleeing the scene. *that's the church bells ringing*, someone says. someone else says, *we're not even close to caspian*. hell, they're screaming without melody, screaming for believers & sins to wash clean. out there in what they believe will be caspian, they'll line the streets to offer what's available.

DJ takes a deep breath & keeps going.

DJ all the churches that rose from this WRECKAGE. the church of circles, claiming, inside everything ends where it begins. the hallways curve & come back. sons & daughters can wander & always be found. there is only a front door & one exit—they are the same. the building is round & its windows pull shafts of light inside, beaming flashlights on the floor, moving as the clouds do. if you were born in the doorway, you will die there. on deathbeds, they celebrate your birth. the church of glass, claiming everything is glass, even the outside walls, except with those you can't see through them. their drawers & cabinets do not hide contents—tables, dictionaries, bullets, condoms, & stray pennies are among other things of consequence. see, you can't enter the sanctuary without emptying your pockets of everything, even lint & paperclips. confession can't be spoken here. no, inside booths, they get written in grease on the walls for the priests to read—the sinner must be exposed as the sin is disclosed. there are two hundred booths, & the sins must stay up for twenty-five hours before the altar boys wipe them clean, & the line goes out the door. by the end of the day there are lists upon lists of sins waiting to be read by the next ones inside. the next ones admit what they've done. watch how sinners look priests in the eyes as they write. no curtain to hide. in here, the face is stitched to the sin. the church of lie, claiming, when you speak, sound carries from your mouth & away to the other end of the room, where the altar is—it's steel &

335

brick in there, & looks like a mason laid it back when men didn't know what was west of them—when the sound returns from the altar it's changed. sometimes, it's smaller, weakened, changing & pulling itself apart chunk by chunk. sometimes, it's big & round, swelling & perspiring. other times, it's got limps & appendages, goiters & sores, & whatever it can collect on its way there & back. see, the thing about this place is how people's mouths part & they speak as if a fire in their throat could beckon a thaw, but it's just words & the place stays cold. even if crowds gathered the place wouldn't warm. this is where stories go to sour, where heroes turn, where rumors turn truth, where cowards dawn capes & masks & dive off to save, where a god & his son go killing sheep & cattle to drink their blood like a couple of hell-bent angels still sore about the fall & the choosing of sides back when lucifer made his move. the ones who enter always change, maybe not religiously, but always their stories do. so, when your words slither back, they come in whispers. one time it came back, whispering, "there's always reasons to kill." the church of lust, claiming, there's lace & skin pulled tight along hallways lit red, but the light is warm & soft. it doesn't blur eyes of the young & eager, sweat readies itself to drip. the light feels like hands running along a back & the air is almost wet, but not quite. the taste lands somewhere between sweat & chocolate. the altar is not a man's room. no, it's behind a curtain. there's moaning, but not sex-moaning or pain. it's more like tongues kicking out mothers of children turning men. on the wall millions of people have carved "i love you" in different forms. it looks like shadows from a projector. the church of fortune, where everything glistens. sleek & glass-like. you swim up to the altar through wet dollar bills. the inside is a pool with dark water. most believers drown. the altar is a towel holder & an elevator to the balcony of a suite. someone has scribbled account numbers on the walls.

DJ takes a long breath. Thinks. Then goes.

DJ but if these leaders find a place & name it caspian, that won't make the stories true & in the final pulse, the center

336

will become noosed. can't you see it cinching daily, & the way the blackest of birds give up their places on wires for the sweating blacktops. we weren't there for it, but we've seen enough from our passes-through to know how it went.

dear survivors,

the desert unlocks & lets us out. lampposts on roadsides carve a path to the coast, & there on the bluff overlooking the town, ankled in the cove, salt smooths the edges of buildings, while in other towns it roughens, tears at the outsides. if you listen you can hear lullabies thick with drawls & humidity.

dear survivors,

some from the lake city bivouacked halfway up the pass in a clearing. there were hundreds living under tents, chopping trees for fires, eating out of cans & from the spigot. though their homes were now lumps in a pile, they started strumming guitars, some radio songs, & told jokes. they were not concerned with caspian. "this place," one said, "is our home." they were wet with concern. "this place," another said, "needs only what we give." & so, well fed & stocked, they slept when the fires found them.

dear survivors,

all of us can see the bridge. the fog is rising off the bay, but we can still see the pilings & wire stretch across. later, our bodies breach the water. if we had purpose, we would be here in the dawn scraping what we could from this moment.

SCENE XXIV

The SOFT DIM LIGHT slowly lights the back corner of the stage. DJ is gone. The red light BUZZES on. LOUD POUNDING OFFSTAGE. It goes & goes & goes & goes & goes & goes & goes. A CRASH. STOMPING. A moment. SOLDIERS enter & for a moment look around—it is clearly empty, maybe abandoned.

GENERAL enters.

SOLDIERS wait for his command.

GENERAL simply nods & moves OFFSTAGE.

SOLDIERS immediately begin to tear the room apart. They rip the cords from the walls, tear the equipment from its place & SLAM it to the floor. They crush it with their feet. They use the butts of their guns to smash it more. They tear empty bookshelves down, they kick the wood into splinters. They smash their gun-butts into the walls. They puncture the walls. They keep at it. They tear the lights from their sockets. There are piles & piles of pieces of this room across the floor. We cannot see the floor, just parts of the radio equipment, pieces of the wall, everything. They wade through the mess they made, looking for more to destroy, but there's nothing.

GENERAL enters again. He looks around. Pleased.

SOLDIERS wait for his command.

OFFSTAGE past the ROPES & PULLEYS, beyond the BRICK WALL & THE CATWALK & THE DRESSING ROOMS, where the trees are thick as semi trucks & the ground is soft, there's a big hole between a gathering of CEDARS. A shovel stuck in the earth next to a pile of dirt.

DJ enters with a wheelbarrow full of notebooks, tapes, folders, records, boxes. They wheel it to the hole & begin to flip through each item, reviewing it. Most of them go into the hole. Occasionally, DJ will take something & slide it in the satchel they have hanging at their side.

LEADER enters, taking the last bite of a bagel.

DJ ignores him.

LEADER has tissue stuck in his collar. His makeup is half-done. He looks genuinely surprised to be in the woods. He looks around mesmerized, like, "how did this forest get here?" He stands there chewing. He spots DJ & wanders over, as though they are friendly. He nods a bit & stops in front of the hole.

    LEADER what's all this?

DJ doesn't answer, keeps doing what they're doing.

    LEADER aren't you on soon?

    DJ i'm busy.

DJ keeps at it. LEADER steps closer, squats, & picks up a notebook. He reads a bit.

    LEADER what are you doing? this isn't in the script.

DJ keeps unloading the wheel barrow & filling the hole.

LEADER pulls out a small rolled up stack of papers. Reads.

DJ keeps at it. LEADER keeps at the conversation.

    LEADER yeah it says here that we find you in your little hideout studio & capture & interrogate you about everything you know & that you have been spreading & then we execute you—the light is really cool there, with your red lights & the spotlight slowly increasing on it till it's almost blinding as i build up to my monologue. there's even that organ blaring. i mean, come on.

LEADER looks at the wheelbarrow, now empty. The hole—filled with books, & paper, & other things.

    LEADER you should put that all back on the stage so we can do this scene.

DJ there's nothing for you in here.

LEADER why are you burying it?

DJ need to keep it safe for now.

LEADER right that's what i'm saying. we're supposed to find all this stuff. i think the script says we burn it after you're executed.

LEADER looks at the script again.

LEADER i don't have that page. but i'm pretty sure.

DJ it belongs here now.

LEADER we'll need them onstage though.

DJ this is not for you. you won't learn from it anyway, it's just kindling to you. it belongs in safety, for now.

LEADER it belongs onstage.

DJ is silent.

LEADER but we need to finish *(gestures towards the stage)* this thing & that's the stuff we need to finish it.

Silence.

LEADER i'm just playing a part, man.

DJ we know.

LEADER there's nothing we can do? i mean, i could just go get the guys & we can bring everything back to the stage.

DJ no. i won't let you.

LEADER but...it's a part...ugh.

DJ things change.

LEADER are you coming back to the play?

DJ do i need to?

LEADER hey, there's my monologue & your execution! that's drama. people are waiting for it.

DJ i think i'm done. i think i've outgrown it? you can finish it without me if you want.

LEADER without you? we can't! you're the final…look… there's a monologue. & i get down really close to your face & say some real mean stuff, like deep-seated, hateful stuff, to really beef up the fact that i'm a villain, you know. like my character is a villain. this—i stand up & pace *(does it)* like this. i say something about what real men are, what they do. i say something about real leaders of men. i talk about men. i say something about the usefulness of fear, fear of a leader, & i rail against the fear you've brought & the doubt you've cast into this nation. the harmfulness of that doubt. i say hope is useless unless it's tied to fear or something like that—i need to run my lines again real quick—but then i give you a good kick to the gut & you cower & cry & i win. & we move forward & the nation forgets you & we find caspian & we destroy it because it is a hope of nothingness. it is nothing but what the survivors made it. it is a perception. & we build a new caspian & people flock to it & they become happy or a version of happy. we rise from the struggle. you become a ghost. the hope you spread becomes ether & people are happy & complacent & calm & live in our caspian.

DJ is that really how it ends?

LEADER it's always been that way.

DJ i don't like it.

LEADER you shouldn't. you're dead at the end of it.

DJ are you sure?

LEADER goes to pull out his script. It's gone. Maybe it burns as he reaches for it. There is only ash in his hand. A wind slams through the woods & carries the ashes everywhere, covering them.

DJ i will live through this & you will have no answers & we will march forward & the gates have opened, but they do not call your name. you will not find it, you will be forgotten, but what you've done will not be forgotten they will replace your name with the name of what you've done.

LEADER but that's not the narrative.

DJ things change.

LEADER but we rehearsed this. my soldiers are—

DJ your soldiers are dead…

ONSTAGE the only still-working light flickers. The SOLDIERS & GENERAL lie in piles across the room. They are not moving.

OUTSIDE OF TIME the GHOSTS DANCE.

Across the stage SURVIVORS move.

CHILDREN walk the edges of the stage SINGING.

CHILDREN ba-ba-ba-baaaaaaaaaaaaaaaaaaaaaaaaaaaaaaaaaaaa
aaaaaaaaaaaaaaaaaaaaaaaaaaaaaaaaaaaaaaaaaaaaaaaaaaaaaaaaaaaa

OFFSTAGE, back past the ROPES & PULLEYs, beyond the BRICK WALL & THE CATWALK & THE DRESSING ROOMS, where the trees are thick as trucks & the ground is soft, there's a big hole between a gathering of CEDARS, and the LEADER stands there, watching as DJ shovels dirt, filling the hole.

LEADER huh.

CURTAIN FALLS

dear survivors,

there are forests of birds, walls of them. there isn't a wire left to perch on, & so, there in the city, on a leveled summit, they sit. they know they won't make it through winter, but they're still alive, still feeding on the worms, waiting for someone to open the warehouse across town so they can make their nests for the winter. there is nothing ahead of us, & just over through the pine needles & mud there is salt-water & rocks. we keep hearing that name. "caspian." but we are all the way west & there is nothing more than cities cratered or shoved into the sea, & there are no men of god leading the blind, just people laying claim to whatever they can. the soldiers keep falling on the horizon, & someone keeps talking about the way things were.

if you listen you can hear history under your foundations.

listen. listen. listen.

NOTES

The following is a list of influences, homages, catalysts, thefts, and other connections from throughout the trilogy. I like the idea of trapdoors. When you recognize something it opens a trapdoor to meaning—I borrowed this idea from Sherman Alexie. You may read something and think "Joshua is a thief" or "nice Sunny Day Real Estate reference." I honestly can't remember all of them, and I'm not going to point them out. Maybe this could be a scavenger hunt type thing—if you find the reference, you win a point. If you find things I forgot, you get two points. I will list the sources as specifically as I can. Sometimes it spans a body of work, sometimes it's one song from one album. *(N.B.: I won't list all the biblical and evangelical references, homages, remixes, and critiques, but these books are FULL of them. So you can take one point for every three you find.)*

C   H   A   P   E   L

Joshua Marie Wilkinson, Noah Eli Gordon, Basement Reading Series, Matthew Brown, Bellingham, Judy Jordan, Rodney Jones, Red Robot (of Redding, CA), *No Country for Old Men*, David Gordon Green, John Allis, Mineral, Ernest Hemmingway, *In Praise of Folly*, *The Thin Red Line*, Patrick Dizney, *O Brother, Where Art Thou?*, Jeremy Vincent, Chris Swanson, *LOST*, Jordan Young, Headphones, David Bazan, Pedro the Lion, The Jealous Sound, a dream I had as a kid, ENG 217: Native Indian Literatures, Botch, The Gloria Record, John Ford, a dream I had after I bought an engagement ring, Alexander Jones, a story I heard as a kid about a kid who turns into a tree, Idiot Pilot, Hank Williams Sr., William Jennings, Chad Fox, Kilmer, Iron & Wine, Cursive, The Dreamers, *American Gods*, D'Arcy McNickle.

W   O   L   V   E   S

David Lynch, Sufjan Stevens, Death Cab for Cutie, Stephen King, Haruki Murakami, a Bellingham train, James Bond movies, *The Godfather*, the idea of WHO IS DEATH?, Hush Harbor, 764-Hero, Starflyer 59, Terrence Malick, Wilco, Galway Kinnell, Calvary Chapel Organization, "Awesome God," hymn books, Sharks Keep Moving, Roslyn, Washington, people from church who claimed my friends had demons inside them and prayed for them, *There Will Be Blood*, Sunny Day Real Estate, Glassjaw, Louis Owens, Sherman Alexie, Kilmer, Judy Jordan, *The Village* (seriously!!!), The Strokes, *The Assassination of Jesse James by the Coward Robert Ford*, Damien Jurado, *The X-Files*, Seldom, Western State Hurricanes, The Casket Lottery, *Se7en*, John Cassavetes, Waxwing, Ryan Adams' "1974," *Six Characters in Search of an Author*, Band of Horses.

R   U   L   E

Ten Grand, The Casket Lottery, Joan of Arc, The Velvet Teen, David Bazan, *The Road*, Faux Pas, The Dance Imperative, *Blood Meridian*, *Endgame*, *Waiting for Godot*, the Bush administration, Flannery O'Connor, Roadside Monument, Counting Crows, Polar Bears, *In the Pines*, *Deepstep Come Shining*, Layne Ransom poems, The Baby Lottery, *A Carnage in the Lovetrees*, Jawbreaker, Cursive, The *Dekalog*, Stanley Kubrick, *Two-Lane Blacktop*, *A Happening at Wretched Knob*, *Maraqopa*, *The Pillowman*, Detroit, *A Behanding in Spokane*, *True West*, Alexis Pope, *Bloodletting in Minor Scales [A Canvas in Arms.]*, *Long Day's Journey into Night*, JB, *The Elaborate Entrance of Chad Deity*, David Lynch, *Black Mirror*.

THANK YOUS

Thank you to Tyler Crumrine and Plays Inverse. Thank you for believing in what I do. But most of all thank you for the friendship.

Thank you to J.A. Tyler & Andrew Borgstrom from Mud Luscious Press (RIP). Thank you also to Jared Michael Wahlgren from Gold Wake Press. You first put these books in the world when no one else was interested.

Thank you to those who reviewed *Wolves* and *Chapel*. Thank you to White Knuckle Press and Gold Wake Press for publishing sections as digital chapbooks. Thank you to the editors of journals who published pieces: *Salt Hill, Oranges & Sardines, BlazeVOX, Rougarou, Slope47, kill author, decomP, Bluestem, The New Gnus, Breadcrumb Scabs, Weave, Prick of the Spindle, wtf pwm, Mud Luscious Quarterly, BWOWP, Used Furniture Review, Ghost Ocean, Corium, NAP, Heavy Feather Review, Word Riot, The Bakery, Jelly Bucket, Ghost Proposal,* and *Alice Blue Review.*

Thank you to Oliver de la Paz. Your guidance, support, and commitment as a mentor is beyond what anyone should expect. Because of you I expect more from teachers/mentors. Because of you these books—this trilogy—exists. And because of you I am where I am. Thank you for demanding more from me and for always encouraging me to push further in writing and life. Also, thank you for reading the 40 extra pages I always turned in and for not failing me in our first class together. If you don't hear this enough, you are one of the most lovely human beings.

Thank you to Richard Greenfield. Our friendship has lasted for longer than I would have expected. I will never forget drinking IPAs in your backyard and you yelling about poetry and indie rock! Thank you for reading *Wolves* and helping me find what the book really was. Thank you for your support. Thank you for your friendship.

Thank you to Carmen Giménez Smith. Even though you told me to knock it off with the projects, you demanded more out of these "poems." Your notes and comments helped shape the whole thing.

Thank you to Kaveh Askari, Kate Trueblood, Bruce Beasley, Rus Bradburd, and Connie Voisine.

Thank you to my crew at WWU and CCC, especially Ian Denning, Matthew Holtmeier, Chelsea Wessels, Meg Forajter, Daniel Scott Parker, and Abigail Zimmer.

Extra thanks to Abigail Zimmer and Ian Denning for your friendship and love. Thank you for making books with me. Thank you for being there for me.

Thank you to Beyza. What can I say, kiddo? I'm glad we met and I'm glad you thought I was cool enough for a friendship.

Thank you to my family, in all its forms. Thanks to my friends, in all their forms.

Thank you to my little brother Jordan for introducing me to more than half of the bands and authors I love.

Thank you to my twin, Caleb, for the constant support and encouragement and daily phone calls.

Thank you to Elliot. My favorite scientist! Thank you to Willa. My favorite guitar player! I love you kiddos so much!!!

Thank you to Alexis Flannery Pope. My love. My partner. My wife. Thank you for your support and belief in me. You are everything. I love you.

JOSHUA YOUNG is the author of *Psalms for the Wreckage* (Plays Inverse, 2017), *THE HOLY GHOST PEOPLE* (Plays Inverse, 2014), and, with Alexis Pope, *I Am Heavy w/ Feeling: A Correspondence* (Fog Machine, 2017), as well as three other collections. His work has appeared in *Gulf Coast, Puerto del Sol, Fugue, Court Green,* and *Vinyl,* among others. Young lives in Chicago with two humans.